Marriage and Family in the Plan of God

Christian Heritage Rediscovered

The Series, as the name suggests, is meant to focus on Christian Faith & Living vis-à-vis topics like Literature & Poetry, Indigenous Philosophizing, Ethical response towards Agriculture, Health & Healing, Science & Technology, Ecofeminist Theology, Sociological approach towards Human Rights, Law & Politics, Arts, History of Ideas, Ancient Civilizations, Cultural Contiguity, Religious Cosmologies & Mysticism, Footsteps of famous Theologians, World Peace & Harmony, Global Capitalism, Network Marketing, Cybertheology, Population & Demographics, Epigraphic Studies, Contextualized Education, and many others. We welcome a Mss. on any topic/s mentioned, whether they are original works, scholarly monographs, collections of conference papers, revised dissertations, or translations of historical documents. Through the Series we, the Publishers, are striving to put forward published works that may help Institutions, Academic Bodies, Researchers, Scholars and the World at large in furthering their respective knowledge and understanding on the concerned subject. We welcome your comments on our efforts and further suggestions on how we can foster the upcoming thoughtful theologically grounded books.

Christian Heritage Rediscovered - 11

Marriage and Family in the Plan of God

Reflections of Saint John Paul II

Edited by

Rev. Dr. L. Sahayaraj

Chancellor of the Diocese of Thanjavur

CWI

Christian World Imprints™

First Published in 2014 by

Christian World Imprints™
Christian Publishing & Books from India
H-12 Bali Nagar, **New Delhi-110015**
info@christianworldimprints.com
www.ChristianWorldImprints.com
Phone: +91 11 25465925 Fax: +91 11 25173055

ISBN-13: 978-93-5148-024-2 ISBN-10: 93-5148-024-0

Cataloging in Publication Data--DK
Courtesy: D.K. Agencies (P) Ltd. <docinfo@dkagencies.com>

John Paul II, Pope, 1920-2005.
Marriage and family in the plan of god : reflections of Saint John Paul II / edited by L. Sahayaraj.
p. cm. -- (Christian heritage rediscovered ; 11)
Includes index.
ISBN 9789351480242
ISBN 9351480240

1. Marriage--Religious aspects--Christianity. 2. Families--Religious aspects--Christianity. I. Sahayaraj, L., 1969- II. Title. III. Series: Christian heritage rediscovered ; 11.

DDC 248.844 23

Printed at Chawla Offset Printers

DEDICATION

TO MY LOVING PARENTS
Mr. S. Lourdusamy and Mrs. A. Philomina
who lived 55 years of Joyful and Exemplary Marital Life

FOREWORD

"The marriage covenant, by which a man and a woman establish between themselves a partnership of their whole life, and which of its own very nature is ordered to the well-being of the spouses and to the procreation and upbringing of children, has, between the baptized, been raised Christ the Lord to the dignity of a sacrament" (Canon 1055).

The above mentioned canon clearly pictures the nature of marriage and importance of family. The transmission of human life is a most serious role in which married people collaborate responsibly with God, the Creator. It has always been a source of a great joy to them, even though it sometimes entails many difficulties and hardships.

St. John Paul II in his Apostolic Exhortation "*Familiaris Consortio*" insists on proposing the divine plan in the basic truths of married love and the family. People say, marriage is fixed in heaven. Because when they enter into the covenant of marriage, God Himself is present in their midst. The recent encyclical of Pope Francis, *Lumen fidei*, speaks of the family in the context of a reflection on how faith reveals "just how firm the bonds between people can be when God is present in their midst" (No. 50).

Taking into the consideration of the importance of marriage and the need of the unity of the family, Rev. Dr. L. Sahayaraj has brought out this collective work based on the reflections of St. John Paul II on "Marriage and Family in the Plan of God". A little sweat and the grace of God can work wonders. The effective writing is the child of both. Rev. Dr. L. Sahayaraj has authored many books and holding doctorate both in Canon and Civil law. He is the effective preacher, teacher and writer. At present he is serving at Bishop's house as the Chancellor of the Diocese. He has put his heart and soul to bring out this work done. Since it has become the need of the hour, I strongly believe that it will be very useful for the priests and religious leaders who are guiding the people in their pastoral ministries for the preparation of marriage and for protection.

With my cordial blessings and prayers,

– Most Rev. Dr. M. Devadass Ambrose
Bishop of Thanjavur

PREFACE

Amidst the great dangers which challenged the teachings of Catholic Church on Marriage and Family, Saint John Paul II who was guiding the Church from 1979 to 2005 was continuously and courageously preaching the teachings of the Church on various occasions to protect the institution of marriage and family. He was explaining clearly the Gospel of Christ, the demands of the Church and its consequences in our day-to-today life. His teachings were so clear and authentic that he was called as "Father of the Families".

I have tried to collect all his important thoughts on marriage and family delivered on different occasions for different groups. All through his Pontificate, he had met so many groups of young people, married people and explained to them the importance of the institution of marriage and the concern of the Church for their well being. I have presented his talks logically on five important topics: Preparing for Marriage, Sacrament of Marriage, Language of Love, ie, Conjugal Relationship, Life is Born Out of Love, ie, Parents and Children, and Joyful & Welcoming Houses, ie, Family, as such. These thoughts will illumine our Christian faith and help us to live and protect the institution of marriage courageously. This is my aim that not only the Christians but people & families from all the different faiths may be enlightened by Saint John Paul II.

I thank Most Rev. Dr. M. Devadass Ambrose, Bishop of Thanjavur, for his support and encouragement in my ministry and also for his foreword and blessings for this small venture. I also thank Christian World Imprints who has accepted to bring out this edition in time.

– Rev. Dr. L. Sahayaraj

INTRODUCTION

Illuminated by the faith that gives her an understanding of all the truth concerning the great value of marriage and the family and their deepest meaning, the Church once again feels the pressing need to proclaim the Gospel, that is the "Good news," to all people without exception, in particular to all those who are called to marriage and are preparing for it, to all married couples and parents in the world.

The Church is deeply convinced that only by the acceptance of the Gospel that the hopes of man which he legitimately places in marriage and in the family are capable of being fulfilled.

Willed by God in the very act of creation, marriage and the family are ordained to fulfillment in Christ and have need of His graces in order to be healed from the wounds of sin and restored to their "beginning," that is, to full understanding and the full realization of God's plan.

At a moment of history in which the family is the object of numerous forces that seek to destroy it or in some way to deform it, and aware that the well-being of society and her own good are intimately tied to the good of the family, the Church perceives in a more urgent and compelling way her mission of proclaiming to all people the plan of God on marriage and family, ensuring their full vitality and human and Christian development, and thus contributing to the renewal of society and of the People of God.

(Pope John Paul II, Apostolic Exhortation, *Familiaris Consortio*, No. 3, 22nd November 1983)

CONTENTS

IV. LIFE IS BORN OUT OF LOVE

V. JOYFUL AND WELCOMING HOUSES

I

Preparing for Marriage

Saint John Paul II stresses the importance of preparation of young people for marriage. A marriage cannot be improvised. From their adulthood, the young people are to be prepared for their future responsibilities. The habit of respecting others, loyalty to keep up the promises, being calm at the time of difficulties, mastering the senses, purity of heart and body will not come at once. People are to be trained and prepared to acquire the good qualities.

Period of preparation is to be given importance, because it permits the young people to know each other and their surroundings. Saint John Paul II warns that this period of preparation should not become "Trial period" or "Trail marriages" or 'Living together". Rather this period should become the time for renewing oneself spiritually, enriching oneself with Christian values and developing or maturing oneself to take up the responsibility of living as good catholic spouse and parent. During the period of preparation, one must know the true teaching of the Church so that he/she can face the dangerous and radical challenges of the modern world and new and sinful way of living. The future spouses must try together with righteous conscience and perseverance to engage themselves to live together with conviction and certainty till the end of life.

1

CALL OF LOVE

Christ replies to the young man in the Gospel. He says: "No one is good but God alone". We have already heard what the young man had asked: "Good Teacher, what must I do to inherit eternal life?" How must I act so that my life will have meaning and value? We could translate his question into the language of our own times. In today's context Christ's answer means this: only God is the ultimate source of all values; only he gives the definitive meaning to our human existence.

Only God is good, which means this: in him and him alone all values have their first source and final completion; he is "the Alpha and Omega, the beginning and the end". Only in him, values and their authenticity and definitive confirmation are found. Without him - without the reference to God - the whole world and its values remain as it were suspended in an absolute vacuum. It also loses its transparency, its clarity. Evil is put forward as a good and good itself is rejected. Are we not shown this by the very experience of our own time, wherever God has been removed beyond the limits of evaluations, estimations and actions?

Why is God alone good? Because, He is love. Christ gives this answer in the words of the Gospel, and above all by the witness of his own life and death: "For God so loved the world that He gave His only Son". God is good precisely because he is "love".

As we have said, the question about the value and the meaning of life, forms part of the singular treasure of youth. It comes from the very heart of the riches and the anxieties linked with that plan for life that must be undertaken and carried out. Still more so, when youth is tested by personal suffering, or is profoundly aware of the suffering of others; when it experiences a powerful shock at the sight of the many kinds of evil that exist in the world; finally, when it comes face to face with the mystery of sin, of human iniquity (*mysterium iniquitatis*), Christ's reply is this: "Only God is good"; "only God is love". This reply may seem difficult, but it is firm and it is true; it bears within itself the definitive solution. How much I pray that you, my young friends, may hear Christ's reply in the most personal way possible; that your will and the interior path which enable you to grasp it, accept it and undertake its accomplishment!

Christ meant this in his conversation with the young man. He means the same in his conversation with each of you. When you say: "Good Teacher", he asks: "Why do you call me good? No one is good but God alone". And therefore, the fact that I am good bears witness to God. "He who has seen me has seen the Father". Thus, speaks Christ who is teacher and friend, Christ crucified and risen, always the same yesterday, today and forever.

This is the core, the essential point of the reply to these questions which you young people put to him. Your youthfulness opens different prospects before you; it offers you the plan for the whole of your lives. Hence, the question about values, the meaning of life, truth, good and evil finds its answer in the love of God. When Christ in his reply to you tells you to refer all this to God, at the same time he shows you that the source and foundation of this is in yourselves. For each one of you is the image and likeness of God through the very act of creation. Precisely this image and likeness makes you raise the questions that you must ask yourselves. These questions show how man without God cannot understand himself, and cannot even find fulfillment without God. Jesus Christ came into the world first of all in order to make each one of us aware of this. Without him this fundamental dimension of the truth about man would easily sink into obscurity. "The light has come into the world", "and the darkness has not overcome it'.

(Pope John Paul II's Message to the Youth on 31st May 1985)

2

OFFERING ONESELF DEFINITIVELY

Jesus says to us more: “Blessed are those who are pure in hearts”.

You said yourselves: love between man and woman, between young man and young girl, it is to respect the other in his/her body, his/her heart, his/her freedom; it is to receive him/her with admiration as a gift of God; it is to love him/her differently, with the intention of doing everything to make him/her happy and best; it is to unite among themselves to create a family. The other must be loved for himself/herself, but not as an object of pleasure. Such love is learned patiently; it is in need of sacrifices, it is made to last forever.

On this point, you say that some people are uncertain and shaken by the morals of young people and adults who are in favor of juvenile cohabitation and divorce. I understand that they are in disorders. At the time of Jesus, some also thought to take advantage of the concessions that Moses had seemed to give in loyalty, because of the hardness of hearts. But, Jesus reminded the original plan of God: “that man does not separate what God has joined”. If God demands total fidelity, it is to say that it is possible. If Jesus has made a sacrament, to the image of his indissoluble love for the Church, it is that his grace will never evade.

The Act which unites man and woman into one flesh is so big and so strong that it expresses the total union of two persons; this act loses its meaning outside of this marital union, sealed in the sacrament. Similarly, they cannot live only on probation, nor die on probation; they cannot love each other truly on probation. It would be the premature experience of pleasure with the gift of oneself which is destined to last forever. The problem is to prepare oneself for the gift of himself/herself to the other, at the level of his/her heart and will.

(Pope John Paul II's Message to the Youth of Strabourg, 8th October 1988: Cf. L'Osservatore Romano, 42)

3

SOCIAL IMPORTANCE AND NEED OF THE PREPARATION FOR MARRIAGE

The future of the family passes through its adequate preparation. Here we speak of a value and a requirement of marriage, which is needed not only for the young people called to marriage but also for the entire ecclesial and civil community. Not only the Church, but the entire society can receive the treasure from those who are preparing for marriage: the originality and the fervor of love, the flavor of the beauty, the desire for an open dialog, the hope in the future are a gift for all and a reminder to those already married. It is an invitation to return to the sources of their choice, to the "spring time" of their love.

(Pope John Paul II's Message to the Pontifical Council for Family, 26th May 1984, L'Osservatore Romano, 22)

4

PREPARATION FOR MARRIAGE

More than ever necessary in our times is preparation of young people for marriage and family life. In some countries, it is still the families themselves that, according to ancient customs, ensure the passing on to young people of the values concerning married and family life, and they do this through a gradual process of education or initiation. But, the changes that have taken place within almost all modern societies demand that not only the family but also society and the Church should be involved in the effort of properly preparing young people for their future responsibilities. Many negative phenomena which are today noted with regret in family life derive from the fact that, in the new situations, young people not only lose sight of the correct hierarchy of values but, since they no longer have certain criteria of behavior, they do not know how to face and deal with the new difficulties. But, experience teaches that young people who have been well prepared for family life generally succeed better than others.

This is even more applicable to Christian marriage, which influences the holiness of large numbers of men and women. The Church must therefore promote better and more intensive programs of marriage preparation, in order to eliminate as far as possible the difficulties that many married couples find themselves in, and even more in order to favor positively the establishing and maturing of successful marriages.

Marriage preparation has to be seen and put into practice as a gradual and continuous process. It includes three main stages: remote, proximate and immediate preparation.

Remote preparation begins in early childhood, in that wise family training which leads children to discover themselves as being endowed with a rich and complex psychology and with a particular personality with its own strengths and weaknesses. It is the period when esteem for all authentic human values is instilled, both in interpersonal and in social relationships, with all that this signifies for the formation of character, for the control and right use of one's inclinations, for the manner of regarding and meeting people of the opposite sex, and so on. Also necessary, especially for Christians, is solid spiritual and catechetical formation that will show that marriage is a true vocation and mission, without excluding the possibility of the total gift of self to God in the vocation to the priestly or religious life.

Upon this basis, there will subsequently and gradually be built up the proximate preparation, which from the suitable age and with adequate catechesis, as in a catechumenal process, involves a more specific preparation for the sacraments, as it were, a rediscovery of them. This renewed catechesis of young people and others preparing for Christian marriage is absolutely necessary in order that the sacrament may be celebrated and lived with the right moral and spiritual dispositions. The religious formation of young people should be integrated, at the right moment and in accordance with the various concrete requirements, with a preparation for life as a couple. This preparation will present marriage as an interpersonal relationship of a man and a woman that has to be continually developed, and it will encourage those concerned to study the nature of conjugal sexuality and responsible parenthood, with the essential medical and biological knowledge connected with it. It will also acquaint those concerned with correct methods for the education of children, and will assist them in gaining the basic requisites for well-ordered family life, such as stable work, sufficient financial resources, sensible administration, notions of housekeeping.

Finally, one must not overlook preparation for the family apostolate, for fraternal solidarity and collaboration with other families, for active membership in groups, associations, movements and undertakings set up for the human and Christian benefit of the family.

The immediate preparation for the celebration of the sacrament of Matrimony should take place in the months and weeks immediately preceding the wedding, so as to give a new meaning, content and form to the so-called premarital enquiry required by Canon Law. This preparation is not only necessary in every case, but is also more urgently needed for engaged couples that still manifest shortcomings or difficulties in Christian doctrine and practice.

Among the elements to be instilled in this journey of faith, which is similar to the catechumenate, there must also be a deeper knowledge of the mystery of Christ and the Church, of the meaning of grace and of the responsibility of Christian marriage, as well as preparation for taking an active and conscious part in the rites of the marriage liturgy.

The Christian family and the whole of the ecclesial community should feel involved in the different phases of the preparation for marriage, which have been described only in their broad outlines. It is to be hoped that the Episcopal Conferences, just as they are concerned with appropriate initiatives to help engaged couples to be more aware of the seriousness of their choice and also to help pastors of souls to make sure of the couples' proper dispositions, so they will also take steps to see that there is issued a Directory for the Pastoral Care of the Family. In this they should lay down, in the first place, the minimum content, duration and method of the "Preparation Courses," balancing the different aspects-doctrinal, pedagogical, legal and medical-concerning marriage, and structuring them in such a way that those preparing for marriage will not only receive an intellectual training but will also feel a desire to enter actively into the ecclesial community.

Although one must not underestimate the necessity and obligation of the immediate preparation for marriage-which would happen if dispensations from it were easily given-nevertheless such preparation must always be set forth and put into practice in such a way that omitting it, is not an impediment to the celebration of marriage.

(Pope John Paul II, Apostolic Exhortation, *Familiaris Consortio,* No. 66)

5

TEACHING OF THE CHURCH ON SEXUALITY

You made me know that you often consider the Church as an institution that does nothing but promulgate regulations and laws. You think that the Church places a lot of barriers in different fields: sexuality, ecclesiastical structure, the place of women within the Church. And you come to the conclusion that there is a deep gap between the joy that emanates from the Word of Christ and the sense of oppression that stirs in you with the rigidity of the Church.

Dear friends, let me be very frank with you. I know that you speak in good faith. But are you really sure that you have the idea that Christ fully corresponds to the reality of his person? In the Gospel, Christ gives us a challenge, which calls for a radical change of heart (cf. *Mk* 1, 5), the detachment from the goods of the earth (cf. *Mt* 6, 19-21), the forgiveness of offenses (cf. *Mt* 6, 14-15), to love one's enemies (cf. *Mt* 5, 44), the patient endurance of abuse (cf. *Mt* 5, 39-40), and even to the sacrifice of his life for love of neighbor (cf. *Jn* 15, 13). In particular, with regard to the sexual sphere, the firm position was taken by him in defense of the indissolubility of marriage (cf. *Mt* 19, 3-9) and also against the conviction of simple adultery of the heart (cf. *Mt* 5, 27-28). And how can we not be impressed by the concept of "extricate the eye" or "cut the hand" in the event that such members are at the "scandal" (cf. *Mt* 5, 29-30)?

Having these specific references to the Gospel, how is it realistic to imagine that Christ is "permissive" in the field of matrimonial life, when it comes to abortion, premarital sex, extra-marital relationship and homosexuality? It is certain that "permissive" position in this sphere was not in the primitive Christian community, taught by those who had personally known Christ. It is sufficient to refer here the numerous passages of the Pauline letters that speak on this subject (cf. *Rom* 1: 26 ff; *1 Cor* 6, 9, *Gal* 5, 19). The words of the apostle are clear and firm. And I am inspired of the above words. They remain normative for the Church of all time. In the light of the Gospel, the Church teaches that each man has the right to respect and love. The man is important. In her teaching, the Church does not ever pronounce a judgment on people.

But at the level of principles, it must distinguish good from evil. The permissiveness does not make men happy. Likewise, the consumer society does not bring the joy of the heart. The human being realizes itself only insofar as it knows how to accept the demands that come from his dignity of being created in the "image and likeness of God".

Consequently, today, if the Church says things that they do not like, it is because she feels an obligation to do so. It does so for the sake of loyalty. It would be actually much easier to keep the generality and permissiveness. But she feels it as her duty to preach the Gospel of Jesus Christ, to safeguard the values to the maximum, even at the risk of facing the challenge and criticism of today's world.

Is it not therefore true that the Gospel message is a message of joy? Indeed, it is very true! And how is this possible? The answer lies in one word, a short word, but by the content as vast as the sea. This word is "love". The rigor of the precept and the joy of the heart can be reconciled with each other perfectly, if the person who does is motivated by love. One who loves is not afraid of sacrifice; He looks at sacrifice rather as the most convincing proof of the authenticity of his love. Is this not the experience you do yourself towards the person you love? No matter how demanding are requests that it offers, you don't try hard to fulfill them, and the sacrifice that this requirement will cost becomes a source of joy for you.

(Pope John Paul II's Message to the Young People of Amersfoort on 14th May 1985: Cf. L'Osservatore Romano, 22)

6

FEAR OF ACCEPTING THE DEFINITE PLAN OF GOD

Many young people are afraid to consider their own life as a plan of definitive choice and of God. This is, in generous terms, because of this culture which is found in the rich countries. There is a sort of fear to think, to hope and to act in a grand manner. Going far away from the religious concept of life and the refusal to accept the existence of God and to have a specific relationship with God, make man lose his support and sometimes his faith and hope.

(Message of Pope John Paul II to the Young People at Turin on 3rd September 1988: Cf. L'Osservatore Romano, 38)

7

TRIAL MARRIAGES

The first example of an irregular situation is provided by what are called "Trial Marriages," which many people today would like to justify by attributing a certain value to them. But, human reason leads one to see that they are unacceptable, by showing the unconvincing nature of carrying out an "experiment" with human beings, whose dignity demands that they should be always and solely the term of a self-giving love without limitations of time or of any other circumstance.

The Church, for her part, cannot admit such a kind of union, for further and original reasons which derive from faith. For, in the first place, the gift of the body in the sexual relationship is a real symbol of the giving of the whole person: such a giving, moreover, in the present state of things cannot take place with full truth without the concourse of the love of charity, given by Christ. In the second place, marriage between two baptized persons is a real symbol of the union of Christ and the Church, which is not a temporary or "trial" union but one which is eternally faithful. Therefore, between two baptized persons there can exist only an indissoluble marriage.

Such a situation cannot usually be overcome unless the human person, from childhood, with the help of Christ's grace and without fear, has been trained to dominate concupiscence from the beginning and to establish relationships of genuine love with other people. This cannot be secured without a true education in genuine love and in the right use of sexuality, such as to introduce the human person in every aspect, and therefore the bodily aspect too, into the fullness of the mystery of Christ.

It will be very useful to investigate the causes of this phenomenon, including its psychological and sociological aspect, in order to find the proper remedy.

(Pope John Paul II, Apostolic Exhortation,
Familiaris Consortio, No. 80)

8

DE FACTO FREE UNIONS

This means unions without any publicly recognized institutional bond, either civil or religious. This phenomenon, which is becoming ever more frequent, cannot fail to concern pastors of souls, also because it may be based on widely varying factors, the consequences of which may perhaps be containable by suitable action.

Some people consider themselves almost forced into a free union by difficult economic, cultural or religious situations, on the grounds that, if they contracted a regular marriage, they would be exposed to some form of harm, would lose economic advantages, would be discriminated against, etc. In other cases, however, one encounters people who scorn, rebel against or reject society, the institution of the family and the social and political order, or who are solely seeking pleasure. Then there are those who are driven to such situations by extreme ignorance or poverty, sometimes by a conditioning due to situations of real injustice, or by a certain psychological immaturity that makes them uncertain or afraid to enter into a stable and definitive union. In some countries, traditional customs presume that the true and proper marriage will take place only after a period of cohabitation and the birth of the first child.

Each of these elements presents the Church with arduous pastoral problems, by reason of the serious consequences deriving from them, both religious and moral (the loss of the religious sense of marriage seen in the light of the Covenant of God with His people; deprivation of the grace of the sacrament; grave scandal), and also social consequences (the destruction of the concept of the family; the weakening of the sense of fidelity, also towards society; possible psychological damage to the children; the strengthening of selfishness).

The pastors and the ecclesial community should take care and become acquainted with such situations and their actual causes, case by case. They should make tactful and respectful contact with the couples concerned, and enlighten them patiently, correct them charitably and show them the witness of Christian family life, in such a way as to smooth the path for them to regularize their situation. But, above all there must be a campaign of prevention; by fostering the sense of fidelity in the whole moral and religious training of the young; instructing them concerning the conditions and structures that favor such fidelity, without which there is no true freedom; they must be helped to reach spiritual maturity and enabled to understand the rich human and supernatural reality of marriage as a sacrament.

The People of God should also make approaches to the public authorities, in order that the latter may resist these tendencies which divide society and are harmful to the dignity, security and welfare of the citizens as individuals, and they must try to ensure that public opinion is not led to undervalue the institutional importance of marriage and the family. And since in many regions young people are unable to get married properly because of extreme poverty deriving from unjust or inadequate social and economic structures, society and the public authorities should favor legitimate marriage by means of a series of social and political actions which will guarantee a family wage, by issuing directives ensuring housing fitting for family life and by creating opportunities for work and life.

(Pope John Paul II, Apostolic Exhortation,
Familiaris Consortio, No. 81)

9

CATHOLICS WHO HAVE MARRIED ONLY CIVILLY

There are increasing cases of Catholics who for ideological or practical reasons, prefer to contract a merely civil marriage, and who reject or at least defer religious marriage. Their situation cannot of course be likened to that of people simply living together without any bond at all, because in the present case there is at least a certain commitment to a properly defined and probably stable state of life, even though the possibility of a future divorce is often present in the minds of those entering a civil marriage. By seeking public recognition of their bond on the part of the State, such couples show that they are ready to accept not only its advantages but also its obligations. Nevertheless, not even this situation is acceptable to the Church.

The aim of pastoral action will be to make these people understand the need for consistency between their choice of life and the faith that they profess, and to try to do everything possible to induce them to regularize their situation in the light of Christian principle. While treating them with great charity and bringing them into the life of the respective communities, the pastors of the Church will regrettably not be able to admit them to the sacraments.

(Pope John Paul II, Apostolic Exhortation, *Familiaris Consortio*, No. 82)

II

Sacrament of Marriage

For the Christians, the marriage is sacred. In fact, by Baptism, they enter into the union of Christ and the Church. The union of Christ and the Church is the image of marriage. Marriage is the sign of this union. It is a sacrament and grand mystery. As christ, for love gives Himself, completely and unconditionally, to His spouse, i.e., the Church, the spouses should also give themselves to each other, unconditionally for love.

This mutual gift which has the resemblance of that of Christ and the Church is the principal grace of the marriage. It is not grace for a day, but for all through the conjugal life of the couple. By Baptism and Eucharist, they may enjoy this moment of grace and obtain the new forces especially at time of difficulties and tensions.

Relying on this mutual and unconditional gift brings joy to the couple in their marital life. At the final moment of their life, if the spouses witness their fidelity and love, they will be the happiest couple. Saint John Paul II explains this concept of sacrament of marriage in his own words on different occasions.

10

MARRIAGE

STABLE AND UNCONDITIONAL COVENANT

The dignity of the person can be protected only if the *person is considered as sacred* from the moment of conception until death. A person cannot be reduced to the status of a means or a tool of others. Society exists to promote the security and dignity of the person. Therefore, the primary right which society must defend is the *Right to Life*. Whether in the womb or in the final phase of life, a person may never be disposed of in order to make life easier for others. *Every person must be treated as an end in himself or herself.* This is the fundamental principle for all human activity: in health care, in the upbringing of children, in education, in the media. The attitudes of individuals or societies in this regard can be measured by the treatment given to those who for various reasons cannot compete in society - the handicapped, the sick, the aged and the dying. If a society does not treat the human person as sacred, then the formulation of solid ethical principles becomes impossible. The creation of a moral climate which fosters the protection of the weakest members of the human family has also become impossible.

(Pope John Paul II's Message at Uppasala on 9th June 1989: Cf. L'Osservatore Romano, 33)

11

LITRGICAL CELEBRATION OF THE MARRIAGE

Christian marriage normally requires a liturgical celebration expressing in social and community form the essentially ecclesial and sacramental nature of the conjugal covenant between baptized persons.

Inasmuch as it is a sacramental action of sanctification, the celebration of marriage inserted into the liturgy, which is the summit of the Church's action and the source of her sanctifying power, must be *per se* valid, worthy and fruitful. This opens a wide field for pastoral solicitude, in order that the needs deriving from the nature of the conjugal convent, elevated into a sacrament, may be fully met, and also in order that the Church's discipline regarding free consent, impediments, the canonical form and the actual rite of the celebration may be faithfully observed. The celebration should be simple and dignified, according to the norms of the competent authorities of the Church. It is also for them in accordance with concrete circumstances of time and place and in conformity with the norms issued by the Apostolic See to include in the liturgical celebration such elements proper to each culture which serve to express more clearly the profound human and religious significance of the marriage contract, provided that such elements contain nothing that is not in harmony with Christian faith and morality.

Inasmuch as it is a sign, the liturgical celebration should be conducted in such a way as to constitute, also in its external reality, a proclamation of the Word of God and a profession of faith on the part of the community of believers. Pastoral commitment will be expressed here through the intelligent and careful preparation of the Liturgy of the Word and through the education to faith of those participating in the celebration and in the first place the couple being married.

Inasmuch as it is a sacramental action of the Church, the liturgical celebration of marriage should involve the Christian community, with the full, active and responsible participation of all those present, according to the place and task of each individual: the bride and bridegroom, the priest, the witnesses, the relatives, the friends, the other members of the faithful, all of them members of an assembly that manifests and lives the mystery of Christ and His Church. For the celebration of Christian marriage in the sphere of ancestral cultures or traditions, the principles laid down above should be followed.

(Pope John Paul II, Apostolic Exhortation,
Familiaris Consortio, No. 67)

12

CONTENT OF THE LITURGICAL CELEBRATION OF THE MARRIAGE

What a great mission is your father's and mother's! Never forget: "*The future of humanity passes through the family!*" (*Familiaris Consortio*, No. 86). The Pope has come to ask you, in the name of God, a special commitment: to consider with great interest the reality of marriage and the family in this time of trial and of grace; because "marriage is not the result of chance or the product of evolution of unconscious natural forces; it is the wise institution of the Creator to realize in mankind His design of love" (*Humanae Vitae* , No. 8).

Approaching the altar, the couple pronounce the words contained in the ritual of the sacrament of marriage: "I do ... I take you... as a wife (or my husband) and I promise to be faithful in good times and in bad, in sickness and in health, and to love you and honor you all the days of my life" (*Ordo celebrandi matrimonium*, 25). Both of them, who profess these words must be particularly aware of this great truth of faith, which will strengthen the family life. All this constitutes the content of the marriage covenant, by which the meaning of marital life is acquired and the sacrament of marriage is realized. It is *a great sacrament refers to Christ and the Church*, as we read in the Letter to the Ephesians (cf. *Eph* 5: 32).

At the same time, this sacramental union assigns the program and the duties that the bride and bridegroom take for life. Each of the words, *as it is and as it should be*, the '*love*' unites them *in the sight of God*: the presence of God who "loved us first" and that is the source and principle of all true love.

In this program of life the conjugal covenant is contained; it is emphasized clearly that true love does not exist if there is no fidelity. It cannot exist, if it is not sincere. If each one is not giving himself or herself to the other - in the real vocation of marriage - it does not include a full commitment that *lasts up to death*. Only an indissoluble marriage will be lasting and will be a firm support *for the family community*.

In the liturgy of the sacrament it is also asked: "Are you willing to accept responsibly and with love for the children, God may give you, and to educate them according to the law of Christ and His Church?" (*Ordo celebrandi matrimonium*, 24). With it the main characteristics of marital love are completed which *are the very nature of marriage and the will of God*, the author of marriage. By fulfilling this, the couple becomes humanly and in Christian way fertile and open to life.

(Homily of Pope John Paul II at Cordoba, Argentina, 8th April 1987: Cf. L'Osservatore Romano, 19)

13

SACRAMENTAL FORMULA OF THE MARRIAGE

"I take you as my wife"; "I take you as my husband" - these words are at the center of the liturgy of marriage as a sacrament of the Church. These words spoken by the people who are engaged in marriage are inserted in the following formula of consent: "I promise to be faithful to you always, in joy and in sorrow, in sickness and in health, and to love and honor you all the days of my life." With these words, the engaged couple enter the marriage, contract and at the same time receive the sacrament of which both are the ministers. Both of them, the man and the woman, administer the sacrament. They do it before witnesses. The priest is a qualified witness, and at the same time he blesses the marriage and presides over the whole sacramental liturgy. Moreover, all those participating in the marriage rite are in a certain sense witnesses, and some of them (usually two) are called specifically to act as witnesses in an official way. They must testify that the marriage was contracted before God and confirmed by the Church. In the ordinary course of events, sacramental marriage is a public act by means of which two persons, a man and a woman, becomes husband and wife before the ecclesial society, that is, they become the actual subject of the marriage, vocation and life.

Marriage is a sacrament which is contracted by means of the word which is a sacramental sign by reason of its content: "I take you as my wife/as my husband/ and I promise to be always faithful to you, in joy and sorrow, in sickness and in health, and to love you and honor you all the days of my life." However, this sacramental word is, *per se*, merely the sign of the coming into being of marriage. The coming into being of marriage is distinguished from its consummation, to the extent that without this consummation the marriage is not yet constituted in its full reality. The fact that a marriage is juridically contracted but not consummated (*ratum et non-consummatum*) corresponds to the fact that it has not been fully constituted as a marriage. Indeed the very words "I take you as my wife/my husband" refer not only to a determinate reality, but they can be fulfilled only by means of conjugal intercourse. This reality (conjugal intercourse) has moreover been determined from the very beginning by institution of the Creator: "Therefore a man leaves his father and his mother and cleaves to his wife, and they become one flesh" (Gn 2:24).

Thus, the sacrament of marriage as a sign enables us to understand the words of the newlyweds. These words confer a new aspect on their life in a dimension strictly personal and interpersonal (*communio personarum*), on the basis of the language of the body. The administration of the sacrament consists in this: that in the moment of contracting marriage the man and the woman, by means of suitable words and recalling the perennial language of the body, form a sign, an unrepeatable sign, which has also a significance for the future: "all the days of my life," that is to say, until death.

This is a visible and efficacious sign of the covenant with God in Christ, that is, of grace which in this sign should become a part of them as "their own special gift" (according to the expression of 1Cor 7:7).

Expressing this matter in socio-juridical terms, one can say that between the newlyweds there is a stipulated, well-defined conjugal pact. It can also be said that following upon this pact, they have become spouses in a manner socially recognized, and that in this way the family as the fundamental social cell is also constituted in germ.

(General Audience of Pope John Paul II,
5th January 1983: Cf. L'Osservatore Romano, 2)

14

NUPTIAL EXCHANGE OF HEARTS

"I will put my spirit within you". When two human beings, a man and a woman, approach the altar, as ministers of the Sacrament of Matrimony, the Church invokes the Creator. She asks the Holy Spirit to come down on these two who are to become husband and wife and are to begin a family.

They are to live under one roof and create a home. The home is the place where the family lives, the outward framework of that life. But, at the same time there is also the inner mystery of their hearts. People not only live in a home; they also create a home. And they create it by the fact of "living" in each other's hearts: the husband in the wife and the wife in the husband, the children in the parents and the parents in the children. The parental home is the mutual indwelling of human hearts.

So, in the home we see a reflection of the mystery which Christ speaks about in the Cenacle: "If a man loves me, he will keep my word, and my Father will love him, and we will come to him and make our home with him".

Today's liturgy reminds us of the most wonderful image of the community of marriage and the family that was ever written down in Sacred Scripture. It is found in the Letter to the Ephesians, in which Saint Paul says of the union of husband and wife in Christian marriage: "This mystery is a profound one, and I am saying that it refers to Christ and the Church". The love of husband and wife has its model in the love of Christ for the Church and reflects that love in the world. Jesus expressed his love most completely on the Cross, when He sacrificed His own life for the sake of His bride, the Church. The Holy Spirit, which each of us has received in Baptism and Confirmation, makes husbands and wives capable of loving one another with the same sacrificial love. That is why Saint Paul exhorts husbands in the following words: "Husbands, love your wives, as Christ loved the Church and gave Himself up for her, that He might sanctify her". The love of Christ endures forever and is constantly life-giving and fruitful. Likewise, Christian spouses are indissolubly bound to each other in a union which is intended to bring forth and nourish new life.

Every couple approaching the altar to become the ministers of the Sacrament of Matrimony should have this image before their eyes. In this Sacrament, the Church invokes the Holy Spirit that by his sanctifying power he may bring about in the man and woman a spousal change of heart – a change that will become a firm foundation of the marriage covenant.

This spousal change of heart is at the same time a special consecration in marriage. As the man and woman entrust themselves to each other, they consecrate to God their souls and bodies, so that from their union there may develop a mature family community, a communion of love and life.

(Homily of Pope John Paul II at Mumbai,
9th February 1986: Cf. L'Osservatore Romano, 8)

15

LOVE OF THE COUPLE
IMAGE OF THE COVENANT
BETWEEN GOD AND HIS PEOPLE

The communion of love between God and people, a fundamental part of the Revelation and faith experience of Israel, finds a meaningful expression in the marriage covenant which is established between a man and a woman.

For this reason, the central word of Revelation, "God loves His people," is likewise proclaimed through the living and concrete word whereby a man and a woman express their conjugal love. Their bond of love becomes the image and the symbol of the covenant which unites God and His people. And the same sin which can harm the conjugal covenant becomes an image of the infidelity of the people to their God: idolatry is prostitution, infidelity is adultery, and disobedience to the law is abandonment of the spousal love of the Lord. But, the infidelity of Israel does not destroy the eternal fidelity of the Lord, and therefore the ever faithful love of God is put forward as the model of the faithful love which should exist between spouses.

(Pope John Paul II, Apostolic Exhortation, *Familiaris Consortio*, No. 12)

16

IMAGE OF CHRIST AMIDST THE COUPLE

Christian love of the spouses has example in Christ, who gives himself to the Church and who enrolled sacrifice, love, joy and hope in his paschal mystery of death and resurrection.

When the difficulties in marital life are increasing, the solution is not to escape from them, not to break up the marriage. The real solution is contained in the perseverance of the spouses. I know from experience beloved husbands and wives that marital fidelity and mature form reveal the energies of Christian love; create a new family with the novelty of love that has gone through the death and resurrection; marital fidelity is evidence of a true Christian relationship between husband and wife, by which they learn to love each other with the love of Christ; it is the guarantee of a stable and good environment for the formation and well being of the children.

Apostle St. Paul reminded us of the source and model of this conjugal love, which is converted into mutual affection and attention from the bride: "This is a great mystery: but I speak concerning Christ and the Church! However, let each one of you love his own wife as himself, and the woman she respect her husband" (*Eph.* 5: 31-33).

The gaze fixed on Christ strengthens the love of the spouses in this mysterious economy of grace. "No man ever yet hated his own flesh; but nourishes and cherishes it, as Christ does, with the Church" (*Eph.* 5, 29). So the couple learns to look with true love, which translates into delicacy, tenderness, attention to others. They find that each is bound by a personal relationship with God; and both are united by the presence of Christ and the grace of the Holy Spirit to live for one another; economy of life that must be converted into donations to the children and that should be the path of holiness in the family. For this reason, already in Christian antiquity was made to understand this dimension of grace, depicting the image of Christ in the midst of the bride and groom.

(Homily of Pope John Paul II in the Mass for the Families in Panama on 5th March 1983: Cf. L'Osservatore Romano, 11)

17

PRAYER OF TOBIT AND SARAH

Already the young couple from the Book of Tobit gives us an example of building the marriage and family on the rock, on the solid foundation of the Word of God. We listened in this liturgy, the prayer of Tobit and Sarah, which is an excellent introduction to their marriage:

"Lord, God of our fathers, that heaven and earth bless you ... It was you who formed Adam from the dust of the ground, and gave him Eve to help ... if I marry this daughter of Israel, it is not to satisfy my passions, but only a desire to start a family that will bless your name in the following centuries. And Sarah, who implored the merciful help of God, in turn asked: 'May we live happily until our old age, both together'."

Tobit and Sarah know that they have received their life together from God of their fathers. By their union, they continue the work of life. The project of their home is according to the will of the Creator: He created man and woman so that they are one.

(Homily of Pope John Paul II at Port-Louis, Mauritius on 14th October 1989: Cf. L'Osservatore Romano, 47)

18

MARRIAGE BETWEEN CATHOLICS AND OTHER BAPTIZED CHRISTIANS

In your country, there are many *marriages between Catholics and other Baptized Christians.* Sometimes, these couples experience special difficulties. To these families I say: You live in your marriage, the hopes and difficulties of the path to Christian unity. Express that hope in prayer together, in the unity of love. Together invite the Holy Spirit of love into your hearts and into your homes. He will help you to grow in trust and understanding.

(Homily of Pope John Paul II in York, Great Britain on 31st May 1982: Cf. L'Osservatore Romano, 24)

19

REQUIREMENTS FOR THE CHRISTIAN MARRIAGE IN THE CHURCH

Precisely because in the celebration of the sacrament very special attention must be devoted to the moral and spiritual dispositions of those being married, in particular to their faith, we must here deal with a not infrequent difficulty in which the Pastors of the Church can find themselves in the context of our secularized society.

In fact, the faith of the person asking the Church for marriage can exist in different degrees, and it is the primary duty of pastors to rediscover this faith, nourish it and bring it to maturity. But, pastors must also understand the reasons that lead the Church also to admit to the celebration of marriage those who are imperfectly disposed.

The sacrament of Matrimony has this specific element that distinguishes it from all the other sacraments: it is the sacrament of something that was part of the very economy of creation; it is the very conjugal covenant instituted by the Creator "in the beginning." Therefore, the decision of a man and a woman to marry in accordance with this divine plan, that is to say, the decision to commit by their irrevocable conjugal consent their whole lives in indissoluble love and unconditional fidelity, really involves, even if not in a fully conscious way, an attitude of profound obedience to the will of God, an attitude which cannot exist without God's grace. They have thus already begun what is in a true and proper sense a journey towards salvation, a journey which the celebration of the sacrament and the immediate preparation for it can complement and bring to completion, given the uprightness of their intention.

On the other hand, it is true that in some places engaged couples ask to be married in Church for motives which are social rather than genuinely religious. This is not surprising. Marriage, in fact, is not an event that concerns only the persons actually getting married. By its very nature, it is also a social matter, committing the couple being married in the eyes of society. And its celebration has always been an occasion of rejoicing that brings together families and friends. It therefore goes without saying that social as well as personal motives enter into the request to be married in Church.

Nevertheless, it must not be forgotten that these engaged couples, by virtue of their Baptism, are already really sharers in Christ's marriage Covenant with the Church, and that, by their right intention, they have accepted God's plan regarding marriage and therefore, at least implicitly consent to what the Church intends to do when she celebrates marriage. Thus, the fact that motives of a social nature also enter into the request is not enough to justify refusal on the part of pastors. Moreover, as the Second Vatican Council teaches, "the sacraments by words and ritual elements nourish and strengthen faith": that faith towards which the married couples are already journeying by reason of the uprightness of their intention, which Christ's grace certainly does not fail to favor and support.

As for wishing to lay down further criteria for admission to the ecclesial celebration of marriage, criteria that would concern the level of faith of those to be married, this would above all involve grave risks. In the first place, the risk of making unfounded and discriminatory judgments; secondly, the risk of causing doubts about the validity of marriages already celebrated, with grave harm to Christian communities, and new and unjustified anxieties to the consciences of married couples; one would also fall into the danger of calling into question the sacramental nature of many marriages of brethren separated from full communion with the Catholic Church, thus contradicting ecclesial tradition.

However, when in spite of all efforts, engaged couples show that they reject explicitly and formally what the Church intends to do when the marriage of baptized persons is celebrated, the pastor of souls cannot admit them to the celebration of marriage. Inspite, of his reluctance to do so, he has the duty to take note of the situation and to make it clear to those concerned that, in these circumstances, it is not the Church that is placing an obstacle in the way of the celebration that they are asking for, but themselves.

Once more there appears in all its urgency the need for evangelization and catechesis before and after marriage, effected by the whole Christian community, so that every man and woman that gets married celebrates the sacrament of Matrimony not only validly but also fruitfully.

(Pope John Paul II, Apostolic Exhortation, *Familiaris Consortio*, No. 68)

III

Language of Love

Love has its own meaning and sense. It is not only made up of words, but of gestures of affection, attention to the conjugal life and union of physical bodies. It has to be faithful and true. How can be one faithful and true to the other partner, if he/she is in the state of adultery? If we consider the physical union of bodies as having only the natural purpose, then the meaning of love is false, since it does not explain the mutual giving of oneself.

It will be wrong if we generalize the sexual union. If one does sexual act more frequently only as the natural urge, then he/she makes his/her spouse as an object, a thing or a choice to satisfy himself/herself selfishly. If it continues for a long period, then one day, he/she will not find any pleasure in it. In this case, especially, the woman will suffer more, since she will rapidly feel that she is not loved or respected anymore.

Rather, if there is a periodical continence, mutually accepted to follow and for good motives, the meaning of love lasts long and there is an occasion to find more meaningful and various other forms of love. Practicing continence is wise and prudent. When the union of bodies or the sexual union is no more possible or not wanted by both the spouses, the union of the souls, wills or hearts which existed from the beginning of marriage will give more meaning to the life and keep them happy always. Saint John Paul II delves beautifully and clearly on this concept.

20

DIFFERENCE BETWEEN SEXES

OFFERING OF ONESELF AND THE COMPLIMENTARY

The revelation, and at the same time the original discovery of the nuptial meaning of the body, consists in this: it presents man, male and female, in the whole reality and truth of his body and sex ("they were naked") and at the same time in full freedom from any constraint of the body and of sex. The nakedness of our progenitors, interiorly free from shame, seems to bear witness to this. It can be said that, created by Love, endowed in their being with masculinity and femininity, they are both "naked" because they are free with the freedom of the gift.

This freedom lies at the basis of the nuptial meaning of the body. The human body, with its sex, and its masculinity and femininity seen in the very mystery of creation, is not only a source of fruitfulness and procreation, as in the whole natural order. It includes right from the beginning the nuptial attribute, that is, *the capacity of expressing love, that love in which the person becomes a gift* and by means of this gift fulfills the meaning of his being and existence. Let us recall here, the text of the Second Vatican Council which declared that man is the only creature in the visible world that God willed "for his own sake." It then added that man "can fully discover his true self only in a sincere giving of himself".

The root of that original nakedness free from shame, which Genesis 2:25 speaks of, must be sought in that complete truth about man. Man or woman, in the context of their beatifying beginning, is free with the freedom of the gift. To remain in the relationship of the "sincere gift of themselves" and to become such a gift for each other, through the whole of their humanity made of femininity and masculinity (also in relation to that perspective which Genesis 2:24 speaks of), they must be free precisely in this way.

We mean here, freedom especially as *mastery of oneself* (self-control). From this aspect, it is indispensable *in order that man may be able to "give himself,"* that he may become a gift, that he will be able to "fully discover his true self" in "a sincere giving of himself" (referring to the words of the Council). Thus, the words, "They were naked and were not ashamed" can and must be understood as the revelation and at the same time as the rediscovery of freedom. This freedom makes possible and qualifies the nuptial sense of the body.

Genesis 2:25 says even more, however. It indicates the possibility and the characteristic of this mutual "experience of the body." It enables us also to identify that nuptial meaning of the body *in actu*. When we read: "They were naked and were not ashamed," we directly touch its fruits and indirectly touch almost the root of it. Free interiorly from the constraint of their own bodies and sex, free with the freedom of the gift, man and woman *could enjoy the whole truth, the whole self-evidence of man*, just as God - Yahweh had revealed these things to them in the mystery of creation.

This truth about man, which the conciliar text states precisely in the words quoted above, has two main emphasis. The first affirms that man is the only creature in the world that the Creator willed "for his own sake." The second consists in saying that this same man, willed by the Creator in this way right from "the beginning," can find himself only in the disinterested giving of himself. Now, this truth about man, which seems in particular to grasp the original condition connected with the very "beginning" of man in the mystery of creation, can be reread - on the basis of the conciliar text - in both directions. This rereading helps us to understand even more the nuptial meaning of the body. This meaning seems inscribed in the original condition of man and woman (according to Genesis 2:23-25) and in particular in the meaning of their original nakedness.

If, as we have noted, at the root of their nakedness there is the interior freedom of the gift - the disinterested gift of oneself - precisely that gift enables them both, man and woman, *to find one another*, since the Creator willed each of them "for his (her) own sake" (*Gaudium et Spes*, No. 24). Thus man, in the first beatifying meeting, finds the woman, and she finds him. In this way, he accepts her interiorly. He accepts her as she is willed "for her own sake" by the Creator, as she is constituted in the mystery of the image of God through her femininity. Reciprocally, she accepts him in the same way, as he is willed "for his own sake" by the Creator, and constituted by him by means of his masculinity. The revelation and the discovery of the nuptial meaning of the body consist in this. The Yahwist narrative, and in particular Genesis 2:25, enables us to deduce that man, as male and female, enters the world precisely with this awareness of the meaning of the body, of masculinity and femininity.

The human body, oriented interiorly by the sincere gift of the person, reveals not only its masculinity or femininity on the physical plane, but reveals also such a value and such a beauty as to go beyond the purely physical dimension of sexuality. In this manner, awareness of the nuptial meaning of the body, connected with man's masculinity/femininity, is in a way completed. On the one hand, this meaning indicates a particular capacity of expressing love, in which man becomes a gift. On the other hand, the capacity and deep availability for the affirmation of the person corresponds to it. This is, literally, the capacity of living the fact that the other - the woman for the man and the man for the woman - is, by means of the body, someone willed by the Creator for his or her own sake. The person is unique and unrepeatable, someone chosen by Eternal Love.

The affirmation of the person is nothing but acceptance of the gift, which, by means of reciprocity, creates the communion of persons. This communion is constructed from within. It comprises also the whole "exteriority" of man, that is, everything that constitutes the pure and simple nakedness of the body in its masculinity and femininity. Then, as we read in Genesis 2:25, man and woman were not ashamed. The Biblical expression "were not ashamed" directly indicates "the experience" as a subjective dimension.

(Pope John Paul II's General Audience on 16th January 1980: Cf. L'Osservatore Romano, 4)

21

HUMAN BEINGS WERE NOT MEANT TO BE ALONE

This original blessing is linked to a precise plan of God, which His word has just recalled: "*It is not good that the man should be alone; I will make him a helper fit for him*" (Gn 2:18). So it is that in the Book of Genesis, the Sacred Author describes *the fundamental requirement* on which the marital union of man and woman and, with it, the life of the family that flows from it, is based. It is *a requirement of communion*. Human beings were not made for solitude; they bear within themselves a relational vocation, rooted in their spiritual nature. Because of this vocation, they grow to the extent that they enter into relationships with others, fully discovering themselves only in "a sincere giving of self" (*Gaudium et spes,* No. 24).

Purely functional relationships are not enough for human beings. They need *interpersonal relationships* that are rich in inner depth, gratuitousness and self-sacrifice. Fundamental among these are the relationships created in the family: between husband and wife, and between them and their children. The whole great network of human relationships flows from and is continuously reborn from that relationship by which a man and a woman recognize that they are made for one another and decide to join their individual lives in a single project of life: "*Therefore, a man leaves his father and mother and cleaves to his wife, and they become one flesh*" (Gn 2:24).

One flesh! How can we not see the power of this expression? The Biblical term "flesh" calls to mind not only man's bodily nature, but *his overall identity as body and spirit.* What the spouses achieve is not only a joining of bodies, but a true union of their persons. A union which is so deep that it in some way makes them *a reflection of the "We" of the three Divine Persons* in history (cf. *Letter to Families,* No. 8).

Thus, we can understand how much is at stake in Jesus' discussion with the Pharisees in Mark's Gospel. Those who were speaking with Jesus considered this a problem of interpretation of the Mosaic law, which permitted a man to put his wife away, leading to debates on the reasons that could justify it. Jesus rises totally above this legalistic view, going *to the heart of God's plan.* In the law of Moses, he sees a concession to their "hardness of heart". But, it is to this hardness that Jesus is not resigned. And how could he be, having come precisely to dispel it and to offer to man, with Redemption, the strength to overcome the resistance due to sin? He is not afraid to remind them of the original plan: "*From the beginning of creation, God made them male and female*" (Mk 10:6).

(Address of Pope John Paul II to the Families:
Cf. L'*Osservatore Romano*, October 18 2000)

22

LOVING ONESELF AS CHRIST LOVED

The communion between God and His people finds its definitive fulfillment in Jesus Christ, the Bridegroom who loves and gives Himself as the Savior of humanity, uniting it to Himself as His body.

He reveals the original truth of marriage, the truth of the "beginning", and, freeing man from his hardness of heart, He makes man capable of realizing this truth in its entirety.

This revelation reaches its definitive fullness in the gift of love which the Word of God makes to humanity in assuming a human nature, and in the sacrifice which Jesus Christ makes of Himself on the Cross for His bride, the Church. In this sacrifice there is entirely revealed that plan which God has imprinted on the humanity of man and woman since their creation; the marriage of baptized persons thus becomes a real symbol of that new and eternal covenant sanctioned in the blood of Christ. The Spirit which the Lord pours forth gives a new heart, and renders man and woman capable of loving one another as Christ has loved us. Conjugal Love reaches that fullness to which it is interiorly ordained, conjugal charity, which is the proper and specific way in which the spouses participate in and are called to live the very charity of Christ who gave Himself on the Cross.

In a deservedly famous page, Tertullian has well expressed the greatness of this conjugal life in Christ and its beauty: "How can I ever express the happiness of the marriage that is joined together by the Church strengthened by an offering, sealed by a blessing, announced by angels and ratified by the Father? ... How wonderful the bond between two believers with a single hope, a single desire, a single observance, a single service! They are both brethren and both fellow-servants; there is no separation between them in spirit or flesh; in fact they are truly two in one flesh and where the flesh is one, one is the spirit."

Receiving and meditating faithfully on the word of God, the Church has solemnly taught and continues to teach that the marriage of the baptized is one of the seven sacraments of the New Covenant.

Indeed, by means of Baptism, man and woman are definitively placed within the new and eternal covenant, in the spousal covenant of Christ with the Church. And it is because of this indestructible insertion that the intimate community of conjugal life and love, founded by the Creator, is elevated and assumed into the spousal charity of Christ, sustained and enriched by His redeeming power.

By virtue of the sacramentality of their marriage, spouses are bound to one another in the most profoundly indissoluble manner. Their belonging to each other is the real representation, by means of the sacramental sign, of the very relationship of Christ with the Church.

Spouses are therefore the permanent reminder to the Church of what happened on the Cross; they are for one another and for the children witnesses to the salvation in which the sacrament makes them sharers. Of this salvation event marriage, like every sacrament, is a memorial, actuation and prophecy: "As a memorial, the sacrament gives them the grace and duty of commemorating the great works of God and of bearing witness to them before their children. As actuation, it gives them the grace and duty of putting into practice in the present, towards each other and their children, the demands of a love which forgives and redeems. As prophecy, it gives them the grace and duty of living and bearing witness to the hope of the future encounter with Christ."

Like each of the seven sacraments, so also marriage is a real symbol of the event of salvation, but in its own way. "The spouses participate in it as spouses, together, as a couple, so that the first and immediate effect of marriage (*res et sacramentum*) is not supernatural grace itself, but the Christian conjugal bond, a typically Christian communion of two persons because it represents the mystery of Christ's incarnation and the mystery of His covenant. The content of participation in Christ's life is also specific: conjugal love involves a totality, in which all the elements of the person enter - appeal of the body and instinct, power of feeling and affectivity, aspiration of the spirit and of will. It aims at a deeply personal unity, the unity that, beyond union in one flesh, leads to forming one heart and soul; it demands indissolubility and faithfulness in definitive mutual giving; and it is open to fertility (*Humanae vitae*, No. 9). In a word it is a question of the normal characteristics of all natural conjugal love, but with a new significance which not only purifies and strengthens them, but raises them to the extent of making them feel the expression of specifically Christian Values."

(Pope John Paul II, Apostolic Exhortation,
***Familiaris Consortio,* No. 13)**

23

LOVE

SOURCE AND FORCE OF THE COMMUNITY OF FAMILY

The family, which is founded and given life by love, is a community of persons: of husband and wife, of parents and children, of relatives. Its first task is to live with fidelity the reality of communion in a constant effort to develop an authentic community of persons.

The inner principle of that task, its permanent power and its final goal is love: without love the family is not a community of persons and, in the same way, without love the family cannot live, grow and perfect itself as a community of persons. What I wrote in the Encyclical *Redemptor hominis* applies primarily and especially within the family as such: "Man cannot live without love. He remains a being that is incomprehensible for himself, his life is senseless, if love is not revealed to him, if he does not encounter love, if he does not experience it and make it his own, if he does not participate intimately in it."

The love between husband and wife and, in a derivatory and broader way, the love between members of the same family - between parents and children, brothers and sisters and relatives and members of the household - is given life and sustenance by an unceasing inner dynamism leading the family to ever deeper and more intense communion, which is the foundation and soul of the community of marriage and the family.

(Pope John Paul II, Apostolic Exhortation,
Familiaris Consortio, No. 18)

24

UNDIVIDED UNITY OF THE CONJUGAL COMMUNION

The first communion is the one which is established and which develops between husband and wife: by virtue of the covenant of married life, the man and woman "are no longer two but one flesh" and they are called to grow continually in their communion through day-to-day fidelity to their marriage promise of total mutual self-giving.

This conjugal communion sinks its roots in the natural complementarity that exists between man and woman, and is nurtured through the personal willingness of the spouses to share their entire life-project, what they have and what they are: for this reason such communion is the fruit and the sign of a profoundly human need. But, in the Lord Christ God takes up this human need, confirms it, purifies it and elevates it, leading it to perfection through the sacrament of matrimony: the Holy Spirit who is poured out in the sacramental celebration offers Christian couples the gift of a new communion of love that is the living and real image of that unique unity which makes the Church, an indivisible Mystical Body of the Lord Jesus.

The gift of the Spirit is a commandment of life for Christian spouses and at the same time a stimulating impulse so that every day they may progress towards an ever richer union with each other on all levels-of the body, of the character, of the heart, of the intelligence and will, of the soul-revealing in this way to the Church and to the world the new communion of love, given by the grace of Christ.

Such a communion is radically contradicted by polygamy: this, in fact, directly negates the plan of God which was revealed from the beginning, because it is contrary to the equal personal dignity of men and women who in matrimony give themselves with a love that is total and therefore unique and exclusive. As the Second Vatican Council writes: "Firmly established by the Lord, the unity of marriage will radiate from the equal personal dignity of husband and wife, a dignity acknowledged by mutual and total love."

(Pope John Paul II, Apostolic Exhortation,
Familiaris Consortio, No. 19)

25

FIDELITY OF LOVE

IS IT POSSIBLE?

The presence of newly married people moves me particularly, because the family is a great thing. I once wrote in a magazine an article in which jokingly I quoted Montaigne, a famous French writer : "Marriage is like an animal box: those who are outside of it make everything to go inside and those who are inside make everything to go out of it". But after a few days, I received a letter from an old inspector of an Academy who was the author of many books. In that letter he reproached me: "Your Excellency, you have quoted Montaigne wrongly. My wife and I have been married for sixty years, and for us every day is like the first day." And then he quoted me a French poet, whom I quote in my turn: "I love you every day more; today much more than yesterday, but much less than tomorrow". It is the vow which I make for you.

(John Paul I's Homily to the Young Married Couples on 6th September 1978)

26

INDISSOLUBILITY OF THE CONJUGAL UNION

Conjugal communion is characterized not only by its unity but also by its indissolubility: "As a mutual gift of two persons, this intimate union, as well as the good of children, imposes total fidelity on the spouses and argues for an unbreakable oneness between them."

It is a fundamental duty of the Church to reaffirm strongly, as the Synod Fathers did the doctrine of the indissolubility of marriage. To all those who, in our times, consider it too difficult, or indeed impossible, to be bound to one person for the whole of life, and to those caught up in a culture that rejects the indissolubility of marriage and openly mocks the commitment of spouses to fidelity, it is necessary to reconfirm the good news of the definitive nature of that conjugal love that has in Christ, its foundation and strength.

Being rooted in the personal and total self-giving of the couple, and being required by the good of the children, the indissolubility of marriage finds its ultimate truth in the plan that God has manifested in His revelation: He wills and He communicates the indissolubility of marriage as a fruit, a sign and a requirement of the absolutely faithful love that God has for man and that the Lord Jesus has for the Church.

Christ renews the first plan that the Creator inscribed in the hearts of men and women, and in the celebration of the sacrament of matrimony offers a "new heart": thus the couples are not only able to overcome "hardness of heart," but also and above all they are able to share the full and definitive love of Christ, the new and eternal Covenant made flesh. Just as the Lord Jesus is the "faithful witness," the "yes" of the promises of God and thus, the supreme realization of the unconditional faithfulness with which God loves His people, so Christian couples are called to participate truly in the irrevocable indissolubility that binds Christ to the Church; His bride, loved by Him to the end.

The gift of the sacrament is at the same time a vocation and commandment for the Christian spouses, that they may remain faithful to each other forever, beyond every trial and difficulty, in generous obedience to the holy will of the Lord: "What therefore God has joined together, let not man put asunder."

To bear witness to the inestimable value of the indissolubility and fidelity of marriage is one of the most precious and most urgent tasks of Christian couples in our time. So, with all my Brothers who participated in the Synod of Bishops, I praise and encourage those numerous couples who, though encountering no small difficulty, preserve and develop the value of indissolubility: thus, in a humble and courageous manner, they perform the role committed to them of being in the world a "sign"- a small and precious sign, sometimes also subjected to temptation, but always renewed - of the unfailing fidelity with which God and

Jesus Christ love each and every human being. But, it is also proper to recognize the value of the witness of those spouses who, even when abandoned by their partner, with the strength of faith and of Christian hope have not entered a new union: these spouses too give an authentic witness to fidelity, of which the world today has a great need. For this reason, they must be encouraged and helped by the pastors and the faithful of the Church.

(Pope John Paul II, Apostolic Exhortation,
Familiaris Consortio, No. 20)

27

PHYSICAL UNION

EXPRESSION OF THE COMMUNION OF MINDS AND HEARTS

Christian spouses have made promises to share everything they are and everything they have. This is the most daring contract and the most wonderful too!

The union of their bodies, willed by God himself is an expression of profound communion of their minds and hearts, accomplished with as much respect as tenderness, renewed vitality and youthfulness of their solemn commitment, their first "yes".

The union of their characters: to love a human being is to love as he/she is; to love to the point of cultivating in himself/herself un antidote of weaknesses or faults, for example, to be calm and patient if the other partner is notoriously lacking them.

The union of hearts! The nuances that differentiate the love of man and the love of woman are endless. Each partner may demand to be loved as he/she likes. And it is important - from both sides - to give up the secret reproaches which separate hearts. They must put together and unify their joys and, more importantly, their suffering of the heart. But it is equally in the common love of children that the union of hearts is strengthened.

The union of minds and wills! Spouses are also two diverse forces, but combined for their mutual service, in service to their homes, to their social environment and to the service of God. The essential agreement must be manifested in the identification and pursuit of common goals. The most energetic partner must support the will of another, must supplement it at times.

Finally the union of souls! They themselves are united to God! Each spouse must reserve moments of solitude with God, the union of "heart to heart" where the spouse is not the first concern. This indispensable life of the soul united with God is not to be thought of as excluding the sharing of conjugal and family life. In contrast, it kindles the Christian spouses to seek together God, to discover his will and accomplish concretely with illumination and strength drawn from God.

(Homily of Pope John Paul II at Kinshasa on 3rd May 1980)

28

COUPLE ALWAYS AND MORE UNITED

Just as the Christian life requires continual conversion, the married life requires the couple to make *constant and generous efforts to deepen their conjugal communion.* By God's design there exists a natural complementarity and attraction between man and woman. But these still have to be developed and fostered by loving attention to each other's needs, and above all by recourse to the graces received in the Sacrament. The Holy Spirit, the Spirit of Truth and Love, is poured out upon the married couple in a special way in the Sacrament, and he will help them in their desire to overcome personal shortcomings and selfishness and to achieve ever greater communion in Christ.

(Homily of Pope John Paul II for the Young people at Nairobi on 17th August 1985)

29

DUTY OF RESPECTING THE PERSONALITY OF HIS SPOUSE

The term *"beloved"* indicates what is always essential for love, which puts *the second "I" beside one's own "I".* *Friendship - love of friendship* (*amor amicitiae*) - signifies in the Song a particular approach felt and experienced as an interiorly unifying power. The fact that in this approach that female "I" is revealed for her groom as "sister" - and that precisely *as both sister and bride* - has a special eloquence. The expression "sister" speaks of the union in mankind and at the same time of her difference and feminine originality. This is not only with regard to sex, but to the very way of "being person", which means both "being subject" and "being in relationship". The term "sister" seems to express, in a more simple way, the subjectivity of the female "I" in personal relationship with the man, that is, *in the openness of him toward others*, who are understood and perceived as brothers. The sister in a certain sense helps man to identify himself and conceive of himself in this way, constituting for him a kind of challenge in this direction.

The groom in the book of Song of Songs accepts the challenge and seeks the common past, as though he and his woman were descended from the same family circle, as though from infancy they were united by memories of a common home. So, they mutually feel as close as brother and sister who owe their existence to the same mother. From this a specific sense of common belonging follows. The fact that they feel like brother and sister allows them to live their mutual closeness in security and to manifest it, finding support in that, and not fearing the unfair judgment of other men.

Through the name "sister", the groom's words tend to reproduce, I would say, the history of the femininity of the person loved. They see her still in the time of girlhood and they embrace her entire 'I', soul and body, with a *disinterested tenderness*. Hence, *there arises that peace* which the bride speaks of. This is the peace of the body, which in appearance resembles sleep. "Do not arouse, do not stir up love before its own time". This is above all *the peace of the encounter* in mankind as the image of God - and the encounter *by means of a reciprocal and disinterested gift*. "So am I in your eyes, like one who has found peace" (Sg 8:10).

> "You are an *enclosed garden*, my sister, my bride,
> an enclosed garden, *a fountain sealed*" (Sg 4:12).

The metaphors just read, an "enclosed garden, a fountain sealed", reveal *the presence of another vision of the same female "I", master of her own mystery*. We can say that both metaphors express the personal dignity of the woman who as a spiritual subject is in possession and can decide not only on the metaphysical depth, but also on the essential truth and authenticity of the gift of herself, inclined to that union which Genesis speaks of.

The language of metaphors - poetic language - seems to be in this sphere especially appropriate and precise. The "sister bride" is for the man the master of her own mystery as a "garden enclosed" and a "fountain sealed". The language of the body reread in truth keeps pace *with the discovery of the interior inviolability of the person.* At the same time, this discovery expresses the authentic depth of the mutual belonging of the spouses who are aware of belonging to each other, of being destined for each other: "My lover belongs to me and I to him" (Sg 2:16; cf. 6:3).

This awareness of mutual belonging resounds especially on the lips of the bride. In a certain sense, with these words she responds to the groom's words with which he acknowledged her as the master of her own mystery. When the bride says, "My lover belongs to me", she means at the same time, "It is he to whom I entrust myself". Therefore, she says, "and I to him" (Sg 2:16). The words "to me" and "to him" affirm here the whole *depth of that entrustment*, which corresponds to the interior truth of the person.

It likewise corresponds to the nuptial significance of femininity in relation to the male "I", that is, to the language of the body reread in the truth of personal dignity.

The groom states this truth with the metaphors of the "garden enclosed" and the "fountain sealed". The bride answers him with the words of the gift, that is, the entrustment of herself. As master of her own choice she says, "I belong to my lover". The Song of Songs subtly reveals the interior *truth* of this response. The freedom of the gift is the response to the deep awareness of the gift expressed by the groom's words. Through this truth and freedom that love is built up, which we must affirm is authentic love.

(General Audience of Pope John Paul II on 30th May 1984: cf. L'Osservatore Romano, 4th June 1984, page 3)

30

JOY OF RELYING ON THE TENDER CARE OF HER HUSBAND

The author of the Letter to the Ephesians, proclaiming the analogy between the spousal bond which unites Christ and the Church, and that which unites the husband and wife in marriage, writes as follows: "Husbands, love your wives, as Christ loved the Church and gave himself up for her, that he might sanctify her, having cleansed her by the washing of water with the word, that he might present the Church to himself in splendor, without spot or wrinkle or any such thing, that she might be holy and without blemish" (Eph 5:25-27).

It is significant that the image of the Church in splendor is presented in the text quoted as a bride all beautiful in her body. Certainly this is a metaphor. But, it is very eloquent, and it shows how deeply important the body is in the analogy of spousal love. The Church in splendor is "without spot or wrinkle." "Spot" can be understood as a sign of ugliness, and "wrinkle" as a sign of old age or senility. In the metaphorical sense, both terms indicate moral defects and sins. It may be added that in St. Paul the "old man" signifies sinful man (cf. Rom 6:6). Therefore, Christ with his redemptive and spousal love ensures that the Church not only becomes sinless, but remains "eternally young."

The scope of the metaphor is, as may be seen, quite vast. The expressions which refer directly and immediately to the human body, characterizing it in the reciprocal relationships between husband and wife, indicates at the same time, attributes and qualities of the moral, spiritual and supernatural order. This is essential for such an analogy. Therefore, the author of the letter can define the state of the Church in splendor in relation to the state of the body of the bride, free from signs of ugliness or old age ("or any such thing"), simply as holiness and absence of sin. Such is the Church "holy and without blemish." It is obvious then what kind of beauty of the bride is in question, in what sense the Church is the Body of Christ, and in what sense that Body-Bride welcomes the gift of the Bridegroom who "has loved the Church and has given himself for her." Nevertheless, it is significant that St. Paul explains all this reality, which is essentially spiritual and supernatural, by means of the resemblance of the body and of the love whereby husband and wife becomes "one flesh."

In the entire passage of the text cited, the principle of bi-subjectivity is clearly preserved: Christ-Church, Bridegroom-Bride (husband-wife). The author presents the love of Christ for the Church - that love which makes the Church the Body of Christ of which He is the head - as the model of the love of the spouses and as the model of the marriage of the bridegroom and the bride. Love obliges the bridegroom-husband to be solicitous for the welfare of the bride-wife. It commits him to desire her beauty and at the same time to appreciate this beauty and to care for it. Here it is a case of visible beauty, of physical beauty. The bridegroom examines his bride with attention as though in a creative, loving anxiety to find everything that is good and beautiful in her and which he desires for her. That good which he who loves creates, through his love, in the one that is loved, is like a test of that same love and its measure. Giving himself in the most disinterested way, he who loves does so only within the limits of this measure and this control.

When the author of the Letter to the Ephesians - in the succeeding verses of the text (5:28-29) - turns his mind exclusively to the spouses themselves, the analogy of the relationship of Christ to the Church is still more profound and impels him to express himself thus: "Husbands should love their wives as their own bodies" (Eph 5:28). Here, the motive of "one flesh" returns again. In the above-mentioned phrase and in the subsequent phrases it is not only taken up again, but also clarified. If husbands should love their wives as their own bodies, this means that uni-subjectivity is based on bi-subjectivity and does not have a real character but only an intentional one. The wife's body is not the husband's own body, but it must be loved like his own body. It is therefore a question of unity, not in the ontological sense, but in the moral sense: unity through love.

"He who loves his wife loves himself" (Eph 5:28). This phrase confirms that character of unity still more. In a certain sense, love makes the "I" of the other person his own "I": the "I" of the wife, I would say, becomes through love the "I" of the husband. The body is the expression of that "I" and the foundation of its identity. The union of husband and wife in love is expressed also by means of the body.

It is expressed in the reciprocal relationship, even though the author of the letter indicates it especially from the part of the husband. This results from the structure of the total image. The spouses should be "subject to one another out of reverence for Christ" (this was already made evident in the first verses of the text quoted: Eph 5:21-23). However, later on, the husband is above all, he who loves and the wife, on the other hand, is she who is loved. One could even hazard the idea that the wife's submission to her husband, understood in the context of the entire passage of the Letter to the Ephesians (5:21-33), signifies above all the "experience of love." This is all the more so since this submission is related to the image of the submission of the Church to Christ, which certainly consists in experiencing his love. The Church, as bride, being the object of the redemptive love of Christ-Bridegroom, becomes His Body. Being the object of the spousal love of the husband, the wife becomes "one flesh" with him, in a certain sense, his own flesh. The author will repeat this idea once again in the last phrase of the passage analyzed here: "However, let each one of you love his wife as himself" (Eph 5:33).

This is a moral unity, conditioned and constituted by love. Love not only unites the two subjects, but allows them to be mutually interpenetrated, spiritually belonging to one another to such a degree that the author of the letter can affirm: "He who loves his wife loves himself" (Eph 5:28). The "I" becomes in a certain sense the "you" and the "you" the "I" (in a moral sense, that is). Therefore, the continuation of the text analyzed by us reads as follows: "For no man ever hates his own flesh, but nourishes and cherishes it, as Christ does the Church, because we are members of his body" (Eph 5:29-30). The phrase, which initially still referred to the relationships of the married couple, returns successively in an explicit manner to the relationship Christ-Church. So, in the light of that relationship, it leads us to define the sense of the entire phrase. After explaining the character of the relationship of the husband to his own wife by forming "one flesh," the author wishes to reinforce still more his previous statement ("He who loves his wife loves himself"). In a certain sense, he wishes to maintain it by the negation and exclusion of the opposite possibility ("No man ever hates his own flesh"-Eph 5:29). In the union through love the body of the other becomes one's own in the sense that one cares for the welfare of the other's body as he does for his own. It may be said that the above-mentioned words, characterizing the "carnal" love which should unite the spouses, express the most general and at the same time, the most essential content. They seem to speak of this love above all in the language of agape.

The expression according to which man "nourishes and cherishes his own flesh"- that is, that the husband "nourishes and cherishes" the flesh of his wife as his own - seems rather to indicate the solicitude of the parents, the protective relationship, instead of the *conjugal tenderness*. The motivation of this character should be sought in the fact that the author here passes distinctly from the relationship which unites the spouses to the relationship between Christ and the Church. The expressions which refer to the care of the body, and in the first place to its nourishment, to its sustenance, suggest to many Scripture Scholars a reference to the Eucharist with which Christ in his spousal love nourishes the Church. These expressions, even though in a minor key, indicate the specific character of conjugal love, especially that love whereby the spouses become "one flesh." At the same time they help us to understand, at least in a general way, the dignity of the body and the moral imperative to care for its good, for that good which corresponds to its dignity. The comparison with the Church as the Body of Christ, the Body of his redemptive and at the same time spousal love, should leave in the minds of those to whom the Letter to the Ephesians was destined a profound sense of the "sacredness" of the human body in general, and especially in marriage, as the "situation" in which this sense of the sacred determines in an especially profound way, the reciprocal relationships of the persons and, above all, those of the man with the woman, inasmuch as she is wife and mother of their children.

(General Audience of Pope John Paul II on 1st September 1982: cf. L'Osservatore Romano, 6 September 1982, page 3)

31

LOVE IN COURSE OF THE DAYS

The sacraments bring in sanctity into the plan of humanity. They penetrate the soul and body, the femininity and the masculinity of the personal subject, with the power of sanctity. All of this is expressed in the language of the liturgy. It is expressed and manifested meaningfully in it.

The liturgy, liturgical language, *elevates the conjugal pact* of man and woman, based on the language of the body reread in truth, *to the dimensions of mystery*. At the same time, it enables that pact to be fulfilled in these dimensions through the language of the body.

It is precisely the sign of the sacrament of marriage that speaks of this. In liturgical language this sign expresses an interpersonal event, laden with intense personal content, assigned to the two "until death." The sacramental sign signifies not only the *fieri* (the "becoming") - the birth of the marriage - but builds its whole *esse* (its "being"), its duration, both the one and the other as a sacred and sacramental reality, rooted in the dimension of the covenant and grace - in the dimension of creation and redemption. In this way, the liturgical language assigns to both, to the man and woman;

love, fidelity and conjugal honesty through the language of the body. It assigns them the unity and the indissolubility of marriage in the language of the body. *It assigns them as a duty all the sacrum* (holy) *of the person and of the communion of persons*, and likewise their femininity and masculinity - *precisely in this language.*

In this sense, we affirm that liturgical language becomes the language of the body. This signifies a series of acts and duties which form the *spirituality* of marriage, its *ethos*. In the daily life of the spouses these acts become duties, and the duties become acts. These acts - as also the commitments - are of a spiritual nature. Nevertheless, they are expressed at the same time with the language of the body.

The Letter to the Ephesians, in exhorting spouses to defer to each other "out of reverence for Christ" (Eph 5:21), and in urging them, consequently, to show respect in their conjugal relationship, seems to point out - in keeping with Pauline tradition - chastity as a virtue and as a gift.

In this way, *through the virtue* and still more *through the gift* ("life according to the Spirit") *the mutual attraction* of masculinity and femininity *spiritually matures*. Both the man and woman, getting away from concupiscence, find the proper dimension of the freedom of the gift, united to femininity and masculinity in the true spousal significance of the body.

Thus, liturgical language, that is, the language of the sacrament and of the *mysterium*, becomes in their life and in their living together the language of the body in a depth, simplicity and beauty hitherto altogether unknown.

This seems to be the *integral significance* of the sacramental sign of marriage. In that sign - through the language of the body - man and woman encounter the great mystery. This is in order to transfer the light of that mystery - the light of truth and beauty, expressed in liturgical language

- to the language of the body, that is, to the language of the practice of love, fidelity, and conjugal honesty, to the ethos rooted in the redemption of the body (cf. Rom 8:23). In this way, conjugal life becomes in a certain sense liturgical.

(General Audience of Pope John Paul II on 4th July 1984: cf. L'Osservatore Romano, 9th July 1984, page 2)

32

HE SHALL RULE OVER YOU

The statement in Genesis 3:16 is of great significance. It implies a reference to the mutual relationship of man and woman in marriage. It refers to the desire born in the atmosphere of spousal love whereby the woman's "sincere gift of self" is responded to and matched by a corresponding "gift" on the part of the husband. Only on the basis of this principle can both of them, and in particular the woman, "discover themselves" as a true "unity of the two" according to the dignity of the person. The matrimonial union requires respect for and a perfecting of the true personal subjectivity of both of them. *The woman cannot become the "object" of "domination" and male "possession".*

But the words of the Biblical text directly concern original sin and its lasting consequences on men and women. Burdened by hereditary sinfulness, they bear within themselves the constant *"inclination to sin"*, the tendency to go against the moral order which corresponds to the rational nature and dignity of man and woman as persons. This tendency is expressed in *a threefold concupiscence,* which Saint John defines as the lust of the eyes, the lust of the flesh and the pride of life (cf. 1 *Jn* 2:16). The words of the Book of Genesis quoted previously (3: 16) show how this *threefold concupiscence*, the "inclination to sin", will burden the mutual relationship of man and woman.

(Apostolic Letter of John Paul II,
Mulieris dignitatem, No. 10, 5th August 1988)

33

ADULTERY AND ITS CONSEQUENCES

Jesus enters *into the concrete and historical situation of women,* a situation which is *weighed down by the inheritance of sin.* One of the ways in which this inheritance is expressed is habitual discrimination against women in favour of men. This inheritance is rooted within women too. From this point of view, the episode of the woman "caught in adultery" (cf. *Jn* 8:3-11) is particularly eloquent. In the end Jesus says to her: *"Do not sin again",* but first He *evokes an awareness* of sin in the man who accuse her in order to stone her, thereby revealing his profound capacity to see human consciences and actions in their true light. Jesus seems to say to the accusers: Is not this woman, for all her sin, above all a confirmation of your own transgressions, of your "male" injustice, your misdeeds?

This truth is *valid for the whole human race.* The episode recorded in the Gospel of John is repeated in countless similar situations in every period of history. A woman is left alone, exposed to public opinion with "her sin", while behind "her" sin there lurks a man - a sinner, guilty "of the other's sin", indeed equally responsible for it.

And yet his sin escapes notice, it is passed over in silence: he does not appear to be responsible for "the others' sin"! Sometimes, forgetting his own sin, he even makes himself the accuser, as in the case described. How often, in a similar way, *the woman pays* for her own sin (maybe it is she, in some cases, who is guilty of the "others' sin" - the sin of the man), but she alone pays and she pays *all alone!* How often is she abandoned with her pregnancy, when the man, the child's father, is unwilling to accept responsibility for it? And besides the many "unwed mothers" in our society, we also must consider all those who, as a result of various pressures, even on the part of the guilty man, very often "get rid of" the child before it is born. "They get rid of it": but at what price? Public opinion today tries in various ways to "abolish" the evil of this sin. Normally a *woman's conscience does not let her forget* that she has taken the life of her own child, for she cannot destroy that readiness to accept life which marks her "ethos" from the "beginning".

(Apostolic Letter of John Paul II, *Mulieris dignitatem*, No. 10, 5th August 1988)

34

THE CHURCH ALWAYS WORKS TO PROTECT MARRIAGE

To evaluate these new attitudes correctly, one should first of all identify the foundation and limitations of the favor in question. Indeed, this principle easily transcends the presumption of validity since it shapes from within all the canonical norms on marriage, both substantial and procedural. The *support* of marriage, in fact, must inspire the entire activity of the Church, of Pastors, of the faithful and of Civil Society: in a word, of all people of good will. This attitude is not based on a more or less debatable choice but rather on the appreciation of the objective good that every conjugal union and every family represents. It is precisely when the personal and social recognition of so fundamental a good is threatened that the depths of its importance for individuals and communities are discovered.

In light of these considerations, the holy Pastors' duty to defend and foster marriage is quite clear. However, this is also a specific responsibility of all the faithful, indeed, of all men and women and the civil authorities, each according to their own competency.

(Address of John Paul II to the Roman Rota, 2004: Cf. L'Osservatore Romano, February 11 2004)

IV

Life is Born Out of Love

Man's call for love is always inseparably linked to his call for the gift of life. But, since some decades, we hear of call for restriction of child births. In the place of the term "Restriction of child births", the Church prefers to use the term "Responsible fatherhood and motherhood" and for the term "Regulation of births", the Church wants to use "Regulation of the fertility". In fact, the new human being has an inviolable right from the very moment of the conception.

For the problems regarding procreation, the Church uses very strict language against the society which accepts the absolute permissible position. Many people criticize the position of the Church saying that the Church is not up to the expectations of the modern society and it is not responding to the difficulties of the modern society. But, the Church is responding to these problems in a very meaningful way by looking at the integrality of the human being. The transmission of life is a human act and it should be in conformity with the plan of God, the Creator. From Him, the sexuality comes to the human beings. Hence, the natural conditions are to be expected.

A child is the gift of God. In him, the love of parents finds its full dimension and because of the child, they can form a true home. Saint John Paul II explains these ideas more meaningfully and systematically on various occasions.

35

REFUSAL OF A SIMPLE AND SELFISH LIVING TOGETHER

From all the sides, people propose "models" of interpretation of the reality of marriage, which exclude any reference to the higher values of ethics and religion. The practical behavior therefore is not only against the Christian message, but also against the authentic vision of "intimate community of life and love," i.e., the marriage (*Gaudium et Spes*, No. 48).

One of the important tasks of the Christian community is to proclaim boldly, in the context of today's society, the joyful news of the redemption of human love. Christ has 'liberated' the man and the woman and has given the possibility of showing love in truth and fullness. In a society wherein the idols of human beings are just pleasure, comfort and idependence then in that very society there is great danger for the family life because irrespective of closure of the hearts of man & woman there is diminishing value of their conjugal life. The Christian community must challenge a vision of the marital relationship which is not giving importance to the mutual gift of each other without reservation, and proposes the simple coexistence of two lovers, who are ultimately concerned only about themselves.

(Address of Pope John Paul II to the Christian Consultors on Family on 29th November 1980)

36

LOVE AND LIFE

The family is a "community in communion", above all, the conjugal community is in communion. As we read in the Book of Genesis (1:28), God created man in his image: calling him to existence out of love, he called him at the same time to love. Since God is love and man is created in His image, the vocation to love has been, so to speak, organically inscribed in this image, that is, in the humanity of man, whom God created as male and female. And the realization of this image is the deep truth of conjugal communion which makes family communion possible at the root.

With the vocation to love, in fact, there is inseparably connected the vocation to the gift of life. The Church has always taught this inseparable connection: conjugal love is the source of human life, and the gift of human life requires conjugal love at its origin. It is in light of this relationship, set up by God that we understand how the family community can be in communion only when it is the place where love generates life and life springs from love. Neither of these two realities, love and life, would be authentic if they were separated: conjugal love would not exist according to the whole measure of its truth, nor would human life have an origin worthy of its unique grandeur. In a word, the conjugal community would not be in full communion nor, consequently, would it be able to make the family community be in communion.

(Pope John Paul II's Message to the Participants of the Congress on the family on 7th December 1981)

37

A CHILD REFLECTS THE LIVING LOVE OF HIS PARENTS

According to the plan of God, marriage is the foundation of the wider community of the family, since the very institution of marriage and conjugal love are ordained to the procreation and education of children, in whom they find their crowning.

In its most profound reality, love is essentially a gift; and conjugal love, while leading the spouses to the reciprocal "knowledge" which makes them "one flesh," does not end with the couple, because it makes them capable of the greatest possible gift, the gift by which they become cooperators with God for giving life to a new human person. Thus, the couple, while giving themselves to one another, give not just themselves but also the reality of children, who are a living reflection of their love, a permanent sign of conjugal unity and a living and inseparable synthesis of their being a father and a mother.

When they become parents, spouses receive from God the gift of a new responsibility. Their parental love is called to become for the children the visible sign of the very love of God, 'from whom every family in heaven and on earth is named.'"

It must not be forgotten however that, even when procreation is not possible, conjugal life does not for this reason lose its value. Physical sterility in fact can be for spouses, the occasion for other important services to the life of other human person, for example, adoption, various forms of educational work, and assistance to other families and to poor or handicapped children.

(Pope John Paul II, Apostolic Exhortation,
Familiaris Consortio, No. 14)

38

COOPERATORS IN THE LOVE OF GOD, THE CREATOR

With the creation of man and woman in His own image and likeness, God crowns and brings to perfection the work of His hands: He calls them to a special sharing in His love and in His power as Creator and Father, through their free and responsible cooperation in transmitting the gift of human life: "God blessed them, and God said to them, 'Be fruitful and multiply, and fill the earth and subdue it'."

Thus, the fundamental task of the family is to serve life, to actualize in history the original blessing of the Creator- that of transmitting by procreation the divine image from person to person.

Fecundity is the fruit and the sign of conjugal love, the living testimony of the full reciprocal self-giving of the spouses: "While not making the other purposes of matrimony of less account, the true practice of conjugal love, and the whole meaning of the family life which results from it, have this aim: that the couple be ready with stout hearts to cooperate with the love of the Creator and the Savior, who through them will enlarge and enrich His own family day by day."

However, the fruitfulness of conjugal love is not restricted solely to the procreation of children, even understood in its specifically human dimension: it is enlarged and enriched by all those fruits of moral, spiritual and supernatural life which the father and mother are called to hand on to their children, and through the children to the Church and to the World.

(Pope John Paul II, Apostolic Exhortation,
Familiaris Consortio, No. 28)

39

MOTHERHOOD

In order to share this "vision", we must once again *seek a deeper understanding of the truth about the human person* recalled by the Second Vatican Council. The human being - both male and female - is the only being in the world which God willed for its own sake. The human being is a person, a subject who decides for himself. At the same time, man "cannot fully find himself except through a sincere gift of self".39 It has already been said that this description, indeed this definition of the person, corresponds to the fundamental Biblical truth about the creation of the human being - man and woman - in the image and likeness of God. This is not a purely theoretical interpretation, nor an abstract definition, for it *gives an essential indication of what it means to be human,* while emphasizing *the value of the gift of self, the gift of the person.* In this vision of the person we also find the essence of that "ethos" which, together with the truth of creation, will be fully developed by the books of Revelation, particularly the Gospels.

This truth about the person also opens up *the path to a full understanding of women's motherhood.* Motherhood is the fruit of the marriage, union of a man and woman, of that Biblical "knowledge" which corresponds to the "union of the two in one flesh" (cf. *Gen* 2:24). This brings about - on the woman's part - a special "gift of self", as an expression of that spousal love whereby the two are united to each other so closely that they become "one flesh". Biblical "knowledge" is achieved in accordance with the truth of the person only when the mutual self-giving is not distorted either by the desire of the man to become the "master" of his wife ("he shall rule over you") or by the woman remaining closed within her own instincts ("your desire shall be for your husband": *Gen* 3:16).

This *mutual gift of the person in marriage* opens to the gift of a new life, *a new human being,* who is also a person in the likeness of his parents. Motherhood implies from the beginning a special openness to the new person: and this is precisely the woman's "part". In this openness, in conceiving and giving birth to a child, the woman "discovers herself through a sincere gift of self". The gift of interior readiness to accept the child and bring it into the world is linked to the marriage union, which - as mentioned earlier - should constitute a special moment in the mutual self-giving both by the woman and the man. According to the Bible, the conception and birth of a new human being are accompanied by the following words of the woman: *"I have brought a man into being with the help of the Lord" (Gen* 4:1).This exclamation of Eve, the "mother of all the living" is repeated every time a new human being comes into the world. It expresses the woman's joy and awareness that she is sharing in the great mystery of eternal generation. The spouses share in the creative power of God!

The woman's motherhood in the period between the baby's conception and birth is a bio-physiological and psychological process which is better understood in our days than in the past, and is the subject of many detailed studies. Scientific analysis fully confirms that the very physical constitution of women is naturally disposed to motherhood - conception, pregnancy and giving birth - which is a consequence of the marriage union with the man. At the same time, this also corresponds to the psycho-physical structure of women. What the different branches of science have to say on this subject is important and useful, provided that it is not limited to an exclusively bio-physiological interpretation of woman and of her motherhood. Such a *"restricted" picture* would go hand in hand with a materialistic concept of the human being and of the world. In such a case, what is truly essential would unfortunately be lost. Motherhood as a human fact and phenomenon, is fully explained on the basis of the truth about the person. Motherhood *is linked to the personal structure of the woman and to the personal dimension of the gift:* "I have brought a man into being with the help of the Lord" (*Gen* 4:1). The Creator grants the parents the gift of a child. On the woman's part, this fact is linked in a special way to "a sincere gift of self". Mary's words at the Annunciation – "Let it be to me according to your word" - signify the woman's readiness for the gift of self and her readiness to accept a new life.

The eternal mystery of generation, which is in God himself, the one and Triune God (cf. *Eph* 3:14-15), is reflected in the woman's motherhood and in the man's fatherhood. Human parenthood is something shared by both the man and the woman. Even if the woman, out of love for her husband, says: "I have given you a child", her words also mean: "This is our child". Although both of them together are parents of their child, *the woman's motherhood constitutes a special "part" in this shared parenthood,* and the most demanding part. Parenthood - even though it belongs to both - is realized much more fully in the woman, especially in the prenatal period. It is the woman who "pays" directly for this shared generation, which literally absorbs the energies of her body and soul. It is therefore, necessary that *the man* be fully aware that in their shared parenthood he owes *a special debt to the woman.* No programme of "equal rights" between women and men is valid unless it takes this fact fully into account.

Motherhood involves a special communion with the mystery of life, as it develops in the woman's womb. The mother is filled with wonder at this mystery of life, and "understands" with unique intuition what is happening inside her. In the light of the "beginning", the mother accepts and loves as a person, the child she is carrying in her womb. This unique contact with the new human being developing within her gives rise to an attitude towards human beings - not only towards her own child, but every human being - which profoundly marks the woman's personality. It is commonly thought that *women* are more capable than men of paying attention *to another person,* and that motherhood develops this predisposition even more. The man - even with all his sharing in parenthood - always remains "outside" the process of pregnancy and the baby's birth; in many ways he has to *learn* his own *"fatherhood" from the mother.* One can say that this is part of the normal human dimension of parenthood, including the stages that follow the birth of the baby, especially the initial period. The child's upbringing, taken as a whole, should include the contribution of both parents: the maternal and paternal contribution. In any event, the mother's contribution is decisive in laying the foundation for a new human personality.

(Apostolic Letter of John Paul II,
***Mulieris dignitatem*, No. 18, 5th August 1988)**

40

CHALLENGE OF MORAL PRINCIPLES

It is true that you are daily faced with incomprehension or with the challenge of ethical principles which are fundamental to the life and development of each individual of the couple and the family. Today's world gives little importance to marital fidelity and even to the institution of marriage. In claiming the freedom to accept or refuse the fatherhood and motherhood, one comes to divert it from its meaning the exercise of the responsibility of couples, certainly legitimate, but on condition that it does not do violence to the human condition which is the gift of God.

Here also, unfortunately, some do not respect the life of the already conceived child, and declare themselves master of his right to live. All in all, in the contemporary world, they often reduce interpersonal relations to a wish of possession, without true reception of other one. They highlight the self-government of the man and they misread the active sources of love which are in God and in the infinite generosity of God which God gives to those who desire to be loved by Him.

(Pope John Paul II's Address to the Members of the Associations of Catholic Families on 3rd November 1989)

41

TAKING PART IN CREATING THE LIFE

But the Church firmly believes that human life, even if weak and suffering, is always a splendid gift of God's goodness. Against the pessimism and selfishness which cast a shadow over the world, the Church stands for life: in each human life she sees the splendor of that "Yes," that "Amen," who is Christ Himself. To the "No" which assails and afflicts the world, she replies with this living "Yes," thus defending the human person and the world from all who plot against and harm life.

The Church is called upon to manifest anew to everyone, with clear and stronger conviction, her will to promote human life by every means and to defend it against all attacks, in whatever condition or state of development it is found.

Thus, the Church condemns as a grave offense against human dignity and justice all those activities of governments or other public authorities which attempt to limit in any way the freedom of couples in deciding about children. Consequently, any violence applied by such authorities in favor of contraception or, still worse, of sterilization and procured abortion, must be altogether condemned and forcefully rejected. Likewise, to be denounced as gravely unjust are cases where, in international relations, economic help given for the advancement of peoples is made conditional on programs of contraception, sterilization and procured abortion.

(Pope John Paul II, Apostolic Exhortation, *Familiaris Consortio*, No. 30)

42

ABORTION

VIOLATION OF THE FIRST RIGHT OF THE HUMAN BEING

We cannot fail to take into account the formidable problem of abortion which is, in addition, a very serious violation of the Law of God, the Lord of life, and all at the same time, a no less serious violation of the first fundamental rights of the human being. Many people, even Catholics, adopt "permissive" positions on the statutory plan, under the pretext of ensuring a better health assistance and to avoid the evils which arise from clandestine abortion or problems of the unwanted child, for the social marginalization of single mothers, of the delicate state of health of the woman or even the difficult economic situation of the household.

These attitudes are due to ignorance or the lack of belief that, from the very moment of conception, there is a living being, separate from the mother, and a subject of inviolable rights.

The human and religious dimension of love must lead Christian spouses to a valorisation of more and more of the life and to the consideration that, when they generate a son, the spouses are collaborating closely to the plan of God. The Vatican Council II has clearly expressed on the subject of responsible fatherhood as a source of healthy marital spirituality provided that it has a Christian and ecclesial attitude in the transmission of life as conscious and free act, consistent with the purpose of God, the Creator.

The interpretations reductive - that you must clarify - which tend to make the expression "responsible fatherhood" almost a synonym of the contrary, that is to say, the absence of paternity and maternity: in one word the interpretations which say "no" to life are to be excluded, without hesitation. These are problems which require imperative attention by the pastors.

(Address of Pope John Paul II to the Bishops of Colombia on 11th June 1985)

43

PHYSICAL UNION AND PROCREATION

In the context of a culture which seriously distorts or entirely misinterprets the true meaning of human sexuality, because it separates it from its essential reference to the person, the Church more urgently feels how irreplaceable is her mission of presenting sexuality as a value and task of the whole person, created male and female in the image of God.

In this perspective, the Second Vatican Council clearly affirmed that "when there is a question of harmonizing conjugal love with the responsible transmission of life, the moral aspect of any procedure does not depend solely on sincere intentions or on an evaluation of motives. It must be determined by objective standards. These, based on the nature of the human person and his or her acts, preserve the full sense of mutual self-giving and human procreation in the context of true love. Such a goal cannot be achieved unless the virtue of conjugal chastity is sincerely practiced."

It is precisely by moving from "an integral vision of man and of his vocation, not only his natural and earthly, but also his supernatural and eternal vocation," that Paul VI affirmed that the teaching of the Church "is founded upon the inseparable connection, willed by God and unable to be broken by man on his own initiative, between the two meanings of the conjugal act: the unitive meaning and the procreative meaning." And he concluded by re-emphasizing that there must be excluded as intrinsically immoral "every action which, either in anticipation of the conjugal act, or in its accomplishment, or in the development of its natural consequences, proposes, whether as an end or as a means, to render procreation impossible."

When couples, by means of recourse to contraception, separate these two meanings that God, the Creator has inscribed in the being of man and woman and in the dynamism of their sexual communion, they act as "arbiters" of the divine plan and they "manipulate" and degrade human sexuality-and with it themselves and their married partner-by altering its value of "total" self-giving. Thus, the innate language that expresses the total reciprocal self-giving of husband and wife is overlaid, through contraception, by an objectively contradictory language, namely, that of not giving oneself totally to the other. This leads not only to a positive refusal to be open to life but also to a falsification of the inner truth of conjugal love, which is called upon to give itself in personal totality.

When, instead, by means of recourse to periods of infertility, the couple respect the inseparable connection between the unitive and procreative meanings of human sexuality, they are acting as "ministers" of God's plan and they "benefit from" their sexuality according to the original dynamism of "total" self-giving, without manipulation or alteration.

In the light of the experience of many couples and of the data provided by the different human sciences, theological reflection is able to perceive and is called to study further the difference, both anthropological and moral, between contraception and recourse to the rhythm of the cycle: it is a difference which is much wider and deeper than is usually thought, one which involves in the final analysis two irreconcilable concepts of the human person and of human sexuality. The choice of the natural rhythms involves accepting the cycle of the person, that is the woman, and thereby accepting dialogue, reciprocal respect, shared responsibility and self- control. To accept the cycle and to enter into dialogue means to recognize both the spiritual and corporal character of conjugal communion and to live personal love with its requirement of fidelity. In this context, the couple comes to experience how conjugal communion is enriched with those values of tenderness and affection which constitute the inner soul of human sexuality, in its physical dimension also. In this way, sexuality is respected and promoted in its truly and fully human dimension, and is never "used" as an "object" that, by breaking the personal unity of soul and body, strikes at God's creation itself at the level of the deepest interaction of nature and person.

(Pope John Paul II, Apostolic Exhortation,
Familiaris Consortio, No. 32)

44

RABINDRANATH TAGORE AND MAHATMA GANDHI ON CHILD BIRTH

Though the responsible transmission of life they gladly accept children as a sign of fruitfulness and a gift of God. With the birth of a child, which calls for greater sacrificial love, they find their own loving union deepened and widened to include others. In the words of your own Indian sage, Rabindranath Tagore, they recognize this truth:

"Every baby that is born Brings with it the message That God has not lost faith in mankind".

For the Second Vatican Council, responsible parenthood means that parents should "take into account both their own welfare and that of their children, those already born and those which may be foreseen. For this accounting they will reckon with both the material and spiritual conditions of the times as well as of their state in life, maintaining regard finally for the good of the family community, of temporal society and of the Church herself". The Council goes on to say that "when there is a question of harmonizing conjugal love with the responsible transmission of life, the moral aspect of any procedure does not depend solely on sincere intentions or on an evaluation of motives. It must be determined by objective standards. These, based on the nature of the human person and his acts, preserve the full sense of mutual self-giving and human procreation in the context of true love".

We see in the statements of Mahatma Gandhi certain similarities. While he asserted that "the act of generation should be controlled for the ordered growth of the world", he asked the question: "How is the suspension of procreation to be brought about?" And he answered: "Not by immoral and artificial checks... but by a life of discipline and self-control". And he added: "Moral results can only be produced by moral restraints". This, dear brothers and sisters, is the Church's profound conviction.

Furthermore, it is the role of the family everywhere and of all society to proclaim that all human life is sacred from the moment of conception. It is the task of all mankind to reject whatever wounds, weakens or destroys human life – whatever offends the dignity of any human being.

(Homily of Pope John Paul II in
Bombay (Mumbai) on 9th February 1986)

45

RESPONSIBLE FATHERHOOD AND MOTHERHOOD

We said previously that the principle of conjugal morality, taught by the Church (Second Vatican Council, Paul VI), is the criterion of faithfulness to the divine plan. In conformity with this principle the Encyclical *Humanae Vitae* clearly distinguishes between a morally illicit method of birth regulation or, more precisely, of the regulation of fertility, and one that is morally correct.

In the first place "the direct interruption of the generative process already begun" (abortion) is morally wrong, likewise "direct sterilization" and "any action, which either before, at the moment of, or after sexual intercourse, is specifically intended to prevent procreation", therefore, all contraceptive means. It is however morally lawful to *have "recourse to the infertile periods"* : "If therefore there are reasonable grounds for spacing births, arising from the physical or psychological conditions of husband or wife, or from external circumstances, the Church teaches that then married people may take advantage of the natural cycles immanent in the reproductive system and use their sexual act at precisely those times that are infertile, and in this way control birth without offending moral principles..."

The Encyclical emphasizes particularly that "between the two cases there is an essential difference" and therefore a difference of an ethical nature: "in the first case married couples rightly use a facility provided to them by nature; in the other case, they obstruct the natural development of the generative process".

From this there derive two actions that are ethically different, indeed, even opposed: the natural regulation of fertility is morally correct; contraception is not morally correct. This essential difference between the two actions (modes of acting) concerns their intrinsic ethical character, even though my predecessor Paul VI states that "in each case married couples, for acceptable reasons, are both perfectly clear in their intention to avoid children", and he even writes: "that they mean to make sure that none will be born". In these words, the Encyclical admits that even those who make use of contraceptive practices can be motivated by "acceptable reasons", however, this *does not change the moral character which is based on the very structure of the conjugal act as such.*

It might be observed at this point that married couples who have recourse to the natural regulation of fertility, might do so without the valid reasons spoken of above. This, however, is a *separate ethical problem*, when one treats of the moral sense of "responsible parenthood".

Supposing that the reasons for deciding not to procreate are morally correct, there remains the *moral* problem of the manner of acting in this case, and this is expressed in an act which, according to the doctrine of the Church contained in the Encyclical, possesses its own intrinsic moral qualification, either positive or negative. The first one, positive, corresponds to the "natural" regulation of fertility; the second, negative, corresponds to "artificial contraception".

The whole of the previous discussion is summed up in the *exposition of the doctrine* contained in *Humanae Vitae*, by pointing out its normative and at the same time its pastoral character. In the normative dimension, it is a question of making more precise and clear the moral principles of action; in the pastoral dimension, it is a question especially of pointing out the possibility of acting in accordance with these principles ("the possibility of the observance of the divine law").

We should dwell on the interpretation of the content of the Encyclical. To this end one must view that content, that normative-pastoral ensemble, in the light of the theology of the body as it emerges from the analysis of the Biblical texts.

The theology of the body is not merely a theory, but rather a specific, evangelical, Christian pedagogy of the body. This derives from the character of the Bible, and especially of the Gospel which, as the message of salvation, reveals *man's true good*, for the purpose of modeling, according to the measure of this good, man's earthly life in the perspective of the hope of the future World. The Encyclical *Humanae Vitae*, following this line, responds to the question about the true good of man as a person, as male and female; about that which corresponds to the dignity of man and woman when one treats of the important problem of the transmission of life by married couples.

(General Audience of Pope John Paul II on 8th August 1984: cf. L'Osservatore Romano, 13th August 1984, page 1)

46

PERIODIC CONTINENCE

Continence is part of the more general virtue of temperance. Continence consists in the *capacity to dominate, control and direct drives of a sexual character* (concupiscence of the flesh) and their consequences, in the psychosomatic subjectivity of man. Insofar as it is a constant disposition of the will, this capacity, merits being called a virtue.

The concupiscence of the flesh, and the corresponding desire of a sexual character aroused by it, is expressed with a specific impulse in the sphere of somatic reaction and also with a psycho-emotive excitement of the sensual impulse.

The personal subject, in order to succeed in mastering this impulse and excitement, must be committed to a progressive education in self-control of the will, feelings and emotions. This education must develop beginning with the simplest acts in which it is relatively easy to put the interior decision into practice. As is obvious, this presupposes the clear perception of the values expressed in the law and the consequent formation of firm convictions. If accompanied by the *respective disposition* of the will, these convictions give rise to the corresponding virtue. This is precisely the virtue of continence (self-mastery). This virtue is seen to be the fundamental condition for the reciprocal language of the body to remain in the truth and for the couple to "defer to one another out of reverence for Christ," according to the words of Scripture (Eph 5:21). This "deferring to one another" *means the common concern for the truth of the language of the body*; rather, deferring "out of reverence for Christ" indicates the gift of the fear of God (a gift of the Holy Spirit) which accompanies the virtue of continence.

This is very important for an adequate understanding of the virtue of continence and especially of the so-called "periodic continence" dealt in the Encyclical *Humanae Vitae*. The conviction that *the virtue of continence* is set against the concupiscence of the flesh is correct, but it is not altogether complete. It is not complete especially when we take into account the fact that this virtue does not appear and does not act abstractly and therefore in isolation. But, it always appears and acts, in connection with the other, virtues (*nexus virtutum*), and therefore *in connection with* prudence, justice, fortitude and *above all with charity*.

In the light of these considerations it is easy to understand that continence is not limited to offering resistance to the concupiscence of the flesh. But, through this resistance it *is open likewise to those values, more profound and more mature*, inherent in the spousal significance of the body in its femininity and masculinity, as well as in the authentic freedom of the gift in the reciprocal relations of the persons. Concupiscence of the flesh itself, insofar as it seeks above all carnal and sensual satisfaction, makes man in a certain sense, blind and insensitive to the most profound values that spring from love and which at the same time constitute love in the interior truth that is proper to it.

Linked to power of love

In this way, also the essential character of conjugal chastity is manifested in its organic link with the power of love, which is poured out into the hearts of the married couple along with the consecration of the sacrament of marriage. In addition, it becomes evident that the call directed to the couple that they "defer to one another out of reverence for Christ" (Eph 5:21) seems to open that interior space in which *both become ever more sensitive to the most profound and most mature values* that are connected with the spousal significance of the body and with the true freedom of the gift.

Conjugal chastity (and chastity in general) is manifested at first as the capacity to resist the concupiscence of the flesh. It later gradually reveals itself as a *singular capacity* to perceive, love and practice those meanings of the language of the body which remain altogether unknown to concupiscence itself. Those meanings progressively enrich the marital dialogue of the couple, purify it, deepen it, and at the same time simplify it.

Therefore, that asceticism of continence, which the encyclical speaks of, *does not impoverish affective manifestations* (*Humanae Vitae*, No. 21). But, rather it makes them spiritually more intense and therefore enriches them.

No contradiction

Analyzing continence in this way, in the dynamics proper to this virtue (anthropological, ethical and theological), we see that that apparent contradiction disappears, which is often an objection to the Encyclical *Humanae Vitae* and to the doctrine of the Church on conjugal morality. That is, there would be a contradiction (according to those who offer this objection) between the two meanings of the conjugal act, the unitive meaning and the procreative meaning (*Humanae Vitae*, No. 12), so that if it were not licit to separate them, the couple would be deprived of the right to conjugal union when they could not responsibly be permitted to procreate.

The Encyclical *Humanae Vitae* gives an answer to this apparent contradiction, if one studies it in depth. Pope Paul VI confirms that there is no contradiction but only a difficulty connected with the whole interior situation of the "man of concupiscence." Rather, precisely by reason of this *difficulty, there is assigned to the interior and ascetical commitment of the couple the true order of conjugal life.* In view of this order, they become "strengthened and, one might say, consecrated" (*Humanae Vitae*, No. 25) by the sacrament of marriage.

Adequate meaning

That order of conjugal life means in addition the subjective harmony between responsible parenthood and personal communion, a harmony created by conjugal chastity. The interior fruits of continence mature in it. Through this interior maturing, *the conjugal act itself* acquires the importance and dignity proper to it in its potentially procreative meaning. At the same time, all the affective manifestations acquire an adequate meaning (*Humanae Vitae*, No. 21). They serve to express the personal communion of the couple in proportion to the subjective richness of femininity and masculinity.

Particular affection

In keeping with experience and tradition, the encyclical reveals that the conjugal act is also a "manifestation of affection" (*Humanae Vitae*, No. 16). But it is a "*manifestation of particular affection*" because *at the same time* it has a potentially procreative meaning. As a result, it is oriented to express personal union, but *not only that*. At the same time the encyclical indicates, although indirectly, many manifestations of affection, effective exclusively to express the personal union of the couple.

The role of conjugal chastity, and still more precisely that of continence, lies *not only* in protecting the importance and dignity of the conjugal act in relation to its procreative meaning, *but also* in safeguarding the importance and the dignity proper to the conjugal act as expressive of interpersonal union, revealing to the awareness and the experience of the couple all the other possible manifestations of affection that can express this profound communion of theirs. It is indeed a matter of *not doing harm to the communion of the couple* in the case where for just reasons they should abstain from the conjugal act. Still more, this communion, continually being built up, day by day, through suitable affective manifestations, may constitute *a vast terrain* on which, under suitable conditions, the decision for a morally right conjugal act matures.

(General Audience of Pope John Paul II, 24th October 1984. Cf. L'Osservatore Romano, 29th October 1984, p. 1)

It is often thought that continence causes inner tensions which man must free himself from. In the light of the analyses we have done, continence, understood integrally, is rather the only *way to free man from such tensions*. It means nothing other than the spiritual effort aimed at expressing the "language of the body," not only in truth but also in the authentic richness of the manifestations of affection.

Essential reasons

Is this effort possible? In other words, (and under another aspect) the question returns here about the feasibility of the moral law, recalled and confirmed by *Humanae Vitae*. It constitutes one of the most essential questions (and currently also one of the most urgent ones) in the sphere of the spirituality of marriage.

The Church is totally convinced of the correctness of the principle that affirms responsible fatherhood and motherhood, in the sense explained in previous catecheses. This is not only for demographic reasons but for more essential reasons. *We call that fatherhood and that motherhood responsible which correspond to the personal dignity of the couple* as parents, to the *truth* of their person and of the conjugal *act*. Hence, arises the close and direct relationship that links this dimension with the whole spirituality of marriage.

Pope Paul VI, in *Humanae Vitae*, expressed what had been affirmed elsewhere by many authoritative moralists and scientists, even Non-Catholics, namely, that precisely in this field, so profoundly and essentially human and personal, it is necessary above all to refer to man as a person, the subject who decides by himself, and not to means which make him the object (of manipulations) and depersonalize him. It is therefore, a question here of an authentically humanistic meaning of the development and progress of human civilization.

Is this effort possible? *The* whole *question* of the Encyclical Humanae Vitae is not reduced simply to the biological dimension of human fertility (the question of the "natural cycles of fertility"), *but goes back to the very subjectivity* of man, to that personal "I" through which the person is man or woman.

Already *during the discussion in the Second Vatican Council*, in relation to the chapter of *Gaudium et Spes* on the "Dignity of Marriage and the Family and its Promotion," the necessity was discussed for *a deepened analysis of the reactions* (and also of the emotions) *connected with the mutual influence of masculinity and femininity* on the human subject. This question belongs not so much to biology as to psychology. From biology and psychology it then passes into the sphere of the spirituality of marriage and the family. Here, this question is in close relationship with the way of understanding the virtue of continence, i.e., self-mastery and especially of periodic continence.

Understanding continence

A careful analysis of human psychology allows us to arrive at some other essential affirmations. (Psychology is at the same time a subjective self-analysis and then becomes an analysis of an "object" accessible to human knowledge.) In interpersonal relationships in which the mutual influence of masculinity and femininity is expressed, there is freed *in the psycho-emotive subject* in the human "I," alongside a *reaction* distinguishable as *excitement*, another reaction that can and must be called *emotion*. Although, these two kinds of reaction appear joined, it is possible to distinguish them experimentally and to differentiate them with regard to their content or their object.

The objective difference between the one and the other kind of reaction consists in the fact that the *excitement* is above all corporeal and in this sense sensual. On the other hand, even though aroused by the mutual reaction of masculinity and femininity, emotion refers above all to the other person understood in the person's integrality. We can say that this is an *emotion caused by the person*, in relation to the person's masculinity or femininity.

What we are stating here with regard to the psychology of the mutual reactions of masculinity and femininity helps in understanding the role of the virtue of continence, which we spoke about previously. Continence is not only - and not even principally - *the ability to abstain*, i.e., mastery over the multiple reactions that are interwoven in the mutual influence of masculinity and femininity. Such a role would be defined as negative. But, there is also another role, which we can call positive, of self-mastery. It is *the ability to direct* the respective *reactions*, both as to their content and their character.

It has already been said that the mutual reactions of masculinity and femininity, excitement and emotion, appear not only as two distinct and different experiences of the human "I." But very often they appear joined in the sphere of the same experience as two different elements of that experience. The reciprocal degree to which these two elements appear in a given experience depends on various circumstances of an interior and an exterior nature. At times, one of the elements is clearly prevalent; at other times there is rather a balance between them.

Maintaining the balance

As the ability to direct excitement and emotion in the sphere of the mutual influence of masculinity and femininity, continence has *the essential task to maintain the balance* between the communion in which the couple wish to mutually express only their intimate union and that in which (at least implicitly) they accept responsible parenthood. In fact, on the part of the subject, excitement and emotion can jeopardize the orientation and the character of the mutual language of the body.

Excitement seeks above all to be expressed in the form of sensual and corporeal pleasure. That is, it tends toward *the conjugal act* which (depending on the natural cycles of fertility) includes the possibility of procreation. *Emotion*, on the other hand, caused by another human being as a person, even if in its emotive content it is conditioned by the femininity or masculinity of the "other," does not *per se* tend towards the conjugal act. But, it *limits itself* to other *manifestations of affection*, which express the spousal meaning of the body, and which nevertheless do not include its (potentially) procreative meaning.

It is easy to understand what conclusions arise from this with respect to the question of responsible fatherhood and motherhood. These conclusions are of a moral nature.

(General Audience of Pope John Paul II, 30th October 1984. Cf. L'Osservatore Romano, 5th November 1984, p. 1)

We are continuing the analysis of the virtue of continence in the light of the doctrine contained in the Encyclical *Humanae Vitae*. It is well to recall that the great classics of ethical (and anthropological) thought, both the Pre-Christian ones and the Christian ones (St. Thomas Aquinas), see in the virtue of continence not only the capacity to contain bodily and sensual reactions, but even more the capacity to control and guide man's whole sensual and emotive sphere. In the case under discussion, it is a question of the *capacity to direct the line of excitement* towards its correct development *and also* the line *of emotion itself*, orienting it towards the deepening and interior intensification of its pure and, in a certain sense, disinterested character.

Not an opposition

This differentiation between the line of excitement and the line of emotion is not an opposition. It does not mean that the conjugal act, as a result of excitement, does not at the same time involve the deep emotion of the other person. Certainly it does, or at any rate, *it should not be otherwise.*

In the conjugal act, the intimate union should involve a particular intensification of emotions, or rather the deep emotions, of the other person. This is also contained in Ephesians in the form of an exhortation directed to married couples: "Defer to one another out of reverence for Christ" (Eph 5:21).

The distinction between excitement and emotion, noted in this analysis, proves only *the subjective reactive-emotive richness* of the human "I." This richness excludes any unilateral reduction and enables the virtue of continence to be practiced as a capacity to direct the manifesting of both the excitement and the emotion, aroused by the reciprocal reacting of masculinity and femininity.

Natural method

The virtue of continence, so understood, has an essential role in maintaining the interior balance between the two meanings of the conjugal act, the unitive and the procreative (*Humanae Vitae*, No. 12) in view of a truly responsible fatherhood and motherhood.

The Encyclical *Humanae Vitae* devotes due attention to the biological aspect of the question, that is to say, to the rhythmic character of human fertility. In the light of the encyclical, this "*periodicalness*" can be called a *providential index* for a responsible fatherhood and motherhood. Nevertheless, a question such as this one, which has such a profoundly personalistic and sacramental (theological) meaning, *is not resolved only on this level.*

The encyclical teaches responsible fatherhood and motherhood "as a proof of a mature conjugal love." Therefore, it contains not only the answer to the concrete question that is asked in the sphere of the ethics of married life but, as already has been stated - it also indicates a plan of conjugal spirituality, which we wish at least to outline.

Maintains balance

The correct way of *intending and practicing periodic continence as a virtue* (that is, according to *Humanae Vitae* 21, the "mastery of self") also essentially determines the "naturalness" of the method, called also the "natural method." This is "naturalness" at the level of the person. Therefore, there can be no thought of a mechanical application of biological laws. The knowledge itself of the rhythms of fertility - even though indispensable - still does not create that interior freedom of the gift, which is by its nature explicitly spiritual and depends on man's interior maturity. This freedom presupposes such a capacity to direct the sensual and emotive reactions as to make possible *the giving* of self to the other "I" *on the grounds of* the mature *self-possession* of one's own "I" in its corporeal and emotive subjectivity.

Communion of persons

As we know from the Biblical and Theological analyses we have previously done, the human body in its masculinity and femininity is interiorly ordered to the communion of the persons (*communio personarum*). Its spousal meaning consists in this. The spousal meaning of the body has been distorted, almost at its roots, by concupiscence (especially by the concupiscence of the flesh in the sphere of the threefold concupiscence). The virtue of continence in its mature form gradually reveals the pure aspect of the spousal meaning of the body. In this way, continence develops *the personal communion* of the man and the woman, a communion that *cannot be formed* and developed in the full truth of its possibilities *only on the level of concupiscence*. This is precisely what the Encyclical *Humanae Vitae* affirms. This truth has two aspects: the personalistic and the theological.

(General Audience of Pope John Paul II, 7th November 1984. Cf. L'Osservatore Romano, 12th November 1984, p. 1)

47

VARIOUS MANIFESTATIONS OF AFFECTION

In the spiritual life of married couples the gifts of the Holy Spirit are at work, especially the gift of piety, i.e., the gift of respect for what is a work of God.

This gift, together with love and chastity, helps *to identify* in the sum total of married life *that act* in which, at least potentially, the spousal meaning of the body is linked with the procreative meaning. It leads to understanding, among the possible manifestations of affection, the singular or rather the exceptional significance of that act: its dignity and the consequent serious responsibility connected with it. Therefore, the antithesis of conjugal spirituality is constituted, in a certain sense, by the subjective lack of this understanding which is linked to contraceptive practice and mentality. In addition to everything else, this does enormous harm from the point of view of man's interior culture. The virtues of conjugal chastity, and still more the gift of respect for what comes from God, mold the couple's spirituality *to the purpose of protecting the particular dignity of this act*, of this manifestation of affection. In it, the truth of the language of the body can be expressed only by safeguarding the procreative potential.

Responsible fatherhood and motherhood means the spiritual appraisal - conforming to truth - of the conjugal act in the knowledge and in the will of both spouses. In this manifestation of affection, after considering the interior and external circumstances, especially the biological ones, they express their mature readiness for fatherhood and motherhood.

Respect for the work of God contributes to seeing that the conjugal act does not become diminished and deprived of the interior meaning of married life as a whole - that it *does not become a habit* - and that there is expressed in it a sufficient fullness of personal and ethical content, and also of religious content, that is, veneration for the majesty of the Creator, the only and the ultimate depository of the source of life, and for the spousal love of the Redeemer. All this creates and enlarges, so to speak, the interior space for the mutual freedom of the gift in which there is fully manifested the spousal meaning of masculinity and femininity.

The obstacle to this freedom is presented by the *interior constriction of concupiscence*, directed to the other "I" as an object of pleasure. Respect for what God creates gives freedom from this constriction. It frees from all that reduces the other "I" to a mere object and it strengthens the interior freedom of the gift.

This can happen only through a profound *appreciation of the personal dignity* of both the feminine "I" and the masculine "I" in their shared life. This spiritual appreciation is the fundamental fruit of the gift of the Spirit, which urges the person to respect the work of God. From this appreciation, and therefore indirectly from that gift, all the affectionate manifestations which make up the fabric of remaining faithful to the union of marriage derive their true spousal meaning. This union is expressed through the conjugal act only in given circumstances. But, it can and it must be manifested continually, every day, through various affectionate manifestations, which are determined by the capacity of a disinterested emotion of the "I" in relation to femininity and, reciprocally, in relation to masculinity.

The attitude of *respect for the work of God*, which the Spirit stirs up in the couple, has an enormous significance for those affectionate manifestations. This is because side by side with it there is the capacity for deep satisfaction, admiration, disinterested attention to the visible and at the same time the invisible beauty of femininity and masculinity, and finally a deep appreciation of the disinterested gift of the other.

All this determines the spiritual *identification* of what is male or female, of what is corporeal and at the same time personal. From this spiritual identification there emerges the *awareness of the union through the body*, in safeguarding the interior freedom of the gift. Through the affectionate manifestations the couple helps each other remain faithful to the union. At the same time, these manifestations protect in each of them that deep-rooted peace which is in a certain sense the interior resonance of chastity guided by the gift of respect for what God creates.

This gift involves a profound and universal *attention to the person* in one's masculinity and femininity, thus creating the interior climate suitable for personal communion. That procreation which we describe as responsible, rightly matures only in this climate of the personal communion of the couple.

The Encyclical *Humanae Vitae* enables us to trace an outline of conjugal spirituality. This is the human and supernatural climate in which - taking the "biological" order into consideration and, at the same time, on the basis of chastity sustained by the gift of piety - is formed *the interior harmony of marriage*, in respect for what the encyclical calls "the twofold significance of the conjugal act" (*Humanae Vitae*, No. 12). This harmony means that the couple lives together in the interior truth of the language of the body. The Encyclical *Humanae Vitae* proclaims that the connection between this truth and love is inseparable.

(General Audience of Pope John Paul II, 21st November 1984: Cf. L'Osservatore Romano, 26th November 1984, p. 1)

48

SEXUALITY AND SPIRITUAL LIFE

The information and knowledge of the natural methods for responsible parenthood must be based on a correct anthropology, and therefore require, education about the self-control, and then the estimation of the chastity and the assessment of the spiritual dimension of love, that integrates itself and sublimates the instincts and the inclination of the sentiment. Even the commitment in mortification is designed to deliver a truly personal love, capable of asceticism, mutual understanding and patience.

It is necessary to reflect upon marriage and sexuality in the light of the Paschal mystery of Christ, which imports logically suffering and sacrifice, victory and joy, because it illuminates, purifies, elevates and saves. Pope Paul VI says in his Encyclical *Humanae vitae*: "The right and lawful ordering of birth demands, first of all, that spouses fully recognize and value the true blessings of family life and that they acquire complete mastery over themselves and their emotions. For if with the aid of reason and of free will they are to control their natural drives, there can be no doubt at all of the need for self-denial. Only then will the expression of love, essential to married life, conform to right order. This is especially clear in the practice of periodic continence. Self-discipline of this kind is a shining witness to the chastity of husband and wife and, far from being a hindrance to their love of one another, transforms it by giving it a more truly human character. And if this self-discipline does demand that they persevere in their purpose and efforts, it has at the same time the salutary effect of enabling husband and wife to develop to their personalities and to be enriched with spiritual blessings. For it brings to family life abundant fruits of tranquility and peace. It helps in solving difficulties of other kinds. It fosters in husband and wife thoughtfulness and loving consideration for one another. It helps them to repel inordinate self-love, which is the opposite of charity. It arouses in them a consciousness of their responsibilities. And finally, it confers upon parents a deeper and more effective influence in the education of their children. As their children grow up, they develop a right sense of values and achieve a serene and harmonious use of their mental and physical powers." (No. 21)

The teaching about the natural methods cannot therefore be separated from a clear set of interior life nourished by prayer and trust in God, and also from a continuing education for the recourse to the help of the grace, the frequent use of the sacraments of the Eucharist and Reconciliation, the accountability in the acts of charity. In fact, it is not just a biological and psychological question, but of a whole concept and a practice of life, rooted in the "Word of God", which illumines the nature and destiny of man.

(Address of Pope John Paul II to the Participants in a Course on the Natural Regulation of Fertility on 13th December 1985)

49

SCIENTIFIC RESEARCH AND NATURAL REGULATION OF FERTILITY

We are faced with a huge task: increasing contraceptive means invading the world with the help of great financial means, which are inspired by unmentionable motives, in which respect for man and his deepest values is absent. The Church has courageously in defense of human love, life and moral values. There are brave and capable men of science who, with patience and skill, are finding ways based on more careful observation of the characteristics of human sexuality, which are compatible with the requirements of chastity, and capable of promoting a harmonious, and serene marital cohabitation, while respecting the fundamental principles of the Church.

The work of investigation, training and teaching of natural methods of regulation of fertility is therefore of great importance. I want to say a word of encouragement to all those who work in this field, urging them not to cease from their investigations. It is necessary that the individual groups, dedicated to this noble work, appreciate their work and exchange experiences with each other and the results, avoiding misunderstandings and tensions firmly, that could threaten a work so important and so hard.

Since the conditions of the couples are very different because of the different cultures, races, personal situations, etc., it is providential that several methods exist which may respond better in so many different situations. For this reason it is good that the experts in these matters to know some of these methods in order to suggest or even teach, if necessary, the most appropriate method. The Church, through me, thanks you for the work you do and encourages you to continue.

(Address of Pope John Paul II to the Participants in a Course on the Natural Regulation of Fertility on 3rd July 1982)

50

BE UNCONDITIONALLY PRO-LIFE!

In their primary mission of communicating love to each other, of being co-creators with God of human life, and of transmitting the love of God to their children, parents must know that they are fully supported by the Church and Society. The new evangelization must bring a fuller appreciation of *the family as the primary and most vital foundation of society,* the first school of social virtue and solidarity (*Familiaris Consortio,* No. 42). *As the family goes, so goes the nation!*

The new evangelization must also bring out the truth that "*the Gospel of God's love for man, the Gospel of the dignity of the person and the Gospel of life are a single and indivisible Gospel*" (*Evangelium vitae,* No. 2). As believers, how can we fail to see that abortion, euthanasia and assisted suicide are a terrible rejection of God's gift of life and love? And as believers, how can we fail to feel the duty to surround the sick and those in distress with the warmth of our affection and the support that will help them always to embrace life?

The new evangelization calls for *followers of Christ who are unconditionally pro-life:* who will proclaim, celebrate and serve the Gospel for life in every situation. A sign of hope is the *increasing recognition that the dignity of human life must never be taken away,* even in the case of someone who has done great evil. Modern society has the means of protecting itself, without definitively denying criminals the chance to reform (*Evangelium vitae,* No. 27).

(Address of Pope John Paul II:
Cf. *L'Osservatore Romano*, February 3 1999)

51

ADOPTION IS 'A CONCRETE WAY OF LOVE'

To adopt a child is a great *work of love*. When it is done, much is given, but much is also received. It is a true exchange of gifts.

In this area, unfortunately, our time knows many contradictions. Despite the numerous children who, because of the death or inability of their parents, are left without a family, there are so many couples who decide to have no children for often selfish reasons. Others let themselves be discouraged by economic, social or bureaucratic difficulties. Still others, in the desire to have their "own" child at any cost, go far beyond the legitimate help which medical science can offer procreation, even having recourse to morally reprehensible practices. Regarding these tendencies, it must be said that the norms of moral law are more than mere abstract principles, but safeguard the true good of man, and in this case, the good of the child with respect to the interests of his parents.

As an alternative to these questionable means, the existence of so many children without families suggests *adoption as a concrete way of love*. Families like yours are here to say that this is a possible and beautiful way, despite its difficulties; a way, moreover, which is even more feasible than in the past, in this era of globalization which shortens all distances.

Adopting children, regarding and treating them as one's own children signify recognizing that the relationship between parents and children is not measured only by genetic standards. Procreative love is first and foremost *a gift of self*. There is a form of "procreation" which occurs through acceptance, concern and devotion. The resulting relationship is so intimate and enduring that it is in no way inferior to one based on a biological connection. When this is also juridically protected, as it is in adoption, in a family united by the stable bond of marriage, it assures the child that peaceful atmosphere and that *paternal and maternal* love which he needs for his full human development.

(Address of Pope John Paul II,
Cf. *L'Osservatore Romano*, September 13 2000)

V

Joyful and Welcoming Houses

Marriage is essential to form a house. The love of couple results in procreation and with the children, a beautiful house is built on earth and thus the society is widened. The future and welfare of the society depend upon the family. Every family must become God's home so that each one in the family finds true happiness. Every house is a heaven in which God is the Head. In all societies, family is facing a lot of challenges and the meaning of family is underestimated. In some societies, the joint-families have lost place and families have become very small. Saint John Paul II shows the ways to build up joyful houses in this world.

52

FAMILY

WAY TO TRUE HAPPINESS

It is a necessary reflection and, especially nowadays, an urgent reflection. The family is the first school of humanization of the person, and it teaches people the way of true happiness.

In a family where there is an interpersonal communion of love, the human being learns the truth about himself which is an essential prerequisite for happiness. In a family, in particular, the child can learn essentially that the order of the goods of which I spoke, according to their hierarchy. In a family, one is protected from all that prevent him/her to achieve true happiness, through education on self-control, renunciation and joyful exercise of freedom in the truth.

But, above all, it is in the family that the child must be educated to have communion with God in order to have no true happiness. He must be made aware that there is no true happiness without the communion with God.

(Address of Pope John Paul II to the Participants in the in the International Congress on Family-Happiness on 16th November 1987)

53

THE DESTINY OF THE HUMAN BEING DEPENDS UPON THAT OF THE FAMILY

Many people ask: why are families so important? Why does the Church so insist on the topic of marriage and family? The reason is simple, even if not everyone can understand it: the future of the human person, his happiness, his capacity for giving meaning to life, all depends on the family. The destiny of the human being depends upon that of the family; this is why I never tire of saying that the future of humanity is closely linked to that of the family (*Familiaris consortio*, No. 86). This truth is so obvious that the attitude, unfortunately very widespread, of those who neglect, offend and relativize the value of marriage and the family seems paradoxical.

The vision of the human person, the interpretation of his personal unity in which the physical, intellectual and spiritual dimensions are expressed, the significance of the tenderness of married love and of the generation of life are the focus of an epoch-making debate that is having a profound effect on the condition of families. In the face of this situation, the Church's primary task is to point out the reasons that make the commitment to the family of all Christians urgent and necessary. At the same time, it is the task of families themselves and of all people of good will to do their utmost to ensure that the rights of this fundamental social institution be recognized, for the good of individuals and of the whole of society.

(Address of Pope John Paul II, Cf. L'Osservatore Romano, October 24 2001)

54

FAMILY IS THE PLACE WHERE EVERYONE BEGINS HIS LIFE AND LEARNS TO LIVE IN LOVE

The family is at the beginning of salvation history, but it is also at the beginning of the history of humanity; we can say that it is its essence, because the history of humanity is substantially a love story. We can never forget that "man cannot live without love. He remains a being that is incomprehensible for himself, his life is senseless, if love is not revealed to him, if he does not encounter love, if he does not experience it and make it his own, if he does not participate intimately in it" (*Redemptor hominis*, No. 10; repeated in *Familiaris consortio,* No. 18).

The family revolves around this central nucleus of human life and from it society draws its origin. All too often today, this truth is forgotten, belied and trampled upon. We must therefore maximize the opportunities for study and reflection, the ways to mobilize families, the cultural, social and political initiatives which, with respect for roles and duties, can help those responsible for the common good to act consistently with the truth about man, which primarily involves safeguarding human life, marriage and the family. For some time, the Church in Italy has been working in favour of the family in a cultural perspective that combines pastoral action with a marked presence in the fields of culture and of communication.

(Address of Pope John Paul II, Cf. L'Osservatore Romano, October 24 2001)

55

PARENTS AND CHILDREN

You are looking for a support for your families. You want them to be stable, not to break up; you want them to form those living hearts of love by which man can warm himself every day. Persevering in the sacramental marriage bond, you wish to hand down life to your children, and, together with life, human and Christian education. Each of you, dear parents, feel deeply this great responsibility which is bound to the dignity of the father and of the mother. You know that your own salvation, and the salvation of your children, depends on that.

How am I playing the father's part? What kind of a mother am I? These are the questions that you ask yourselves more than once. You rejoice, and I with you, at all good that is manifested in you, in your families, in your children. I take pleasure with you in their progress at school, in the development of their young consciences. You want them to become really "men". And this, to a large extent, depends on what they acquire in their parents' house. No one can replace you in this work. Society, Nation and the Church are constructed by you or their foundations are laid by you.

(Homily of Pope John Paul II at Torre Spaccata,
Rome on 1st April 1979)

56

CHILDREN'S QUESTIONS ARE AN ECHO OF GOD'S VOICE

In looking at the Holy Family, you, Christian spouses, are prompted to ask yourselves about the tasks that Christ assigns to you in your wonderful and demanding vocation.

Do not children themselves *in a way continually "examine" their parents?* They do so not only with their frequent "whys?", but with their very faces, sometimes smiling, sometimes misty with sadness. It is as if *a question* were inscribed in their whole existence, a question which is expressed in the most varied ways, even in their whims, and which we could put into questions like these: Mama, papa, do you love me? Am I really a gift for you? Do you accept me for what I am? Do you always try to do what is really best for me?

These questions perhaps are asked more with their eyes than in words, but they hold parents to their great responsibility and are in some way an echo of God's voice for them.

Children are "springtime": what does this metaphor chosen for your Jubilee means?

It takes us into that panorama of life, colours, light and song which belongs to the spring season. Children are all of this by nature. They are *the hope that continually blossoms,* a project that starts ever anew, the future that opens without ceasing. They represent the flowering of married love, which is found and strengthened in them. At their birth they bring a *message of life* which in the ultimate analysis refers back to the very Author of life. In need of everything as they are, especially in the first stage of life, they *naturally appeal to our solidarity.*

Not by chance did Jesus invite his disciples to have a child's heart (cf. Mk 10:13-16). Today, dear families, you wish to give thanks for the gift of children and, at the same time, to accept *the message that God sends you through their existence.*

Unfortunately, as we know so well, the situation of children in the world is not always what it should be. In many regions, and paradoxically right in the more prosperous countries, bringing children into the world *has become a decision taken with great hesitation,* well beyond that prudence which is necessarily required for responsible procreation. It could be said that at times children are seen as *more of a threat than a gift.*

And what can we say then of the other sad sight of abused and exploited children, to which I called attention in the *Letter to Children?*

(Address of Pope John Paul II: Cf. *L'Osservatore Romano*, October 18 2000)

57

KNOWING TO SPEAK WITH THEIR CHILDREN

Being a parent brings worries and difficulties, as well as joy and fulfillment. *I would remind you, dear parents: your children are your great treasure.* They love you very much, even if they find it hard at times to express that love. It is a sad reality that due to the pressures of work and the quickening pace of life, many parents find it increasingly difficult to give enough time to their children.

I urge you today: *find opportunities for talking and sharing at a deep level with your children.* Do not let them become strangers living under the same roof. The years spent in the home pass so quickly. They are precious years. Every moment spent with your children will enrich them, and you in turn will find your own lives immeasurably enriched. The future of the Church, the future of humanity itself, depends in great part on the quality of family life and the closeness of family ties nurtured in the home. *The greatness of this nation, and any nation, can be measured by the greatness of its families.*

(Homily of Pope John Paul II at Uppasala, Sweden on 9th June 1989)

58

FORMING THE CHILDREN TO HAVE CONSCIENCE OF THEIR VOCATION

Family is the first and fundamental environment in which the Christian vocation flourishes, forms and *manifests*. As the vocation of Jesus was manifested in the family of Nazareth, so every vocation is born and manifests itself even today, in the family.

The families of our time must always be aware of the main and important duty that they have received from God: to train their children to become aware of the place that God has assigned to each one in this world. Why must they become aware of their vocation? Everyone has a mission to fulfill, that no one else can achieve in his place. Everyone is called, as baptized; as a member of the Church, the city of God; as a member of the city of men; as a builder of society in communion with the brethren; as peacemaker; as a witness of the love of God to men.

(Homily of Pope John Paul II at Cuenca, on 31st January 1985)

59

CHILDREN MUST BE ABLE TO COUNT ON BOTH PARENTS

The situation of children is really *a challenge for society as a whole,* a challenge posed directly to families. No one knows as you do, dear parents, how essential it is for children to be able to count on you, on both of you - fathers and mothers - *in the complementarity of your gifts.* No, it is not a step forward for civilized society to support trends that obscure this elementary truth and even demand to be legally recognized.

Are children not already too heavily penalized by the scourge of divorce? How sad it is for a child to have to divide his love between parents in conflict! So many children *will always bear the psychological scar of the suffering* that their parents' separation caused them.

As for the many broken families, the Church feels called not to express a harsh, detached judgement, but rather to *shed the light of God's word,* accompanied by the witness of his mercy, *on the depths of so many human tragedies.* This is the spirit in which the pastoral care of the family must also address the situation of *divorced and remarried believers*. They are not excluded from the community; they are invited, instead, to share in its life, undertaking a journey of growth in the spirit of what the Gospel requires. The Church, while not concealing from them the truth about the objective moral disorder of their situation and the resulting consequences for sacramental practice, wishes to show them all her maternal closeness.

Be certain of this, Christian spouses: the sacrament of matrimony assures you of the necessary grace to persevere in the mutual love that your children need as much as bread.

(Address of Pope John Paul II:
Cf. *L'Osservatore Romano,* October 18 2000)

60

KNOWING TO FORGIVE

No relationship is as intense and close as marriage and the family formed after marriage, cannot survive without forgiveness “seventy times seven times”. If couples cannot forgive with the tenderness and sensitivity that mercy brings, then they will inevitably begin to see their relationship only in terms of justice, of what is mine and what is yours - emotionally, spiritually and materially - and in terms of real or perceived injustices. This can lead to *estrangement and divorce*, and often develops into a bitter dispute about property and, more tragically, about children. The plight of the children alone should make us realize that the refusal to forgive is not in keeping with the true nature of marriage as God established it and as He wants it to be lived. No doubt some people will object Christ’s teaching on the indissolubility of marriage, as it is upheld by the Church, as it is lacking compassion and understanding. But, what must be seen is the ineffectiveness of divorce, and its ready availability in modern society, to bring mercy and forgiveness and healing to so many couples and their children, in whose troubled lives there remain a brokenness and a suffering that will not go away. The words of the merciful Christ, who fully understands the human heart, remain forever: "What therefore God has joined together, let no man put asunder" (*Mt.* 19, 6).

At the same time, merciful love and forgiveness are never meant to cancel out *a person's right to justice*, even in marriage. In the encyclical to which I referred a moment ago, I said that "properly understood, justice constitutes... the goal of forgiveness. In no passage of the Gospel message does forgiveness or mercy... mean indulgence towards evil, scandals, injury or insult... Reparation for evil and scandal, compensation for injury, and satisfaction for insult are conditions for forgiveness" (John Paul II, *Dives in Misericordia*, 14).

(Homily of Pope John Paul II at
New Orleans on 12th September 1987)

61

SACRAMENT OF RECONCILIATION AND FAMILY LIFE

A marriage that is in crisis; a marriage that from the human point of view is close to ruin; a marriage weighed down by mutual estrangement of the partners can be saved only by the spouses provided that they are able to forgive each other and march with perseverance towards reconciliation. The good relationship between the spouses through reconciliation also applies to the relationship between parents and children and children with their parents. In a family, conflict between young and old, between father or mother and son or daughter, must be resolved in mutual understanding and mutual forgiveness.

Adolescents, mothers and fathers should never be too proud or too stubborn, so as that reconciliation may not be possible when there is a discussion. Do not be stubborn and do not bear a grudge when it comes to resolving a dispute. However, it is an essential part of reconciliation with God through good personal confession, since any injury done to our neighbor is also an offense to God. So, do not exclude the reconciliation between God and men. Find out the means of salvation which is called confession and the inner peace which only the Lord can give.

Marriage and family can respond to their highest Christian vocation only through the regular practice of conversion and personal confession. Reconciliation through confession should have its permanent place in the lives of spouses and family members.

(Pope John Paul II's Homily at Liechtenstein, Switzerland on 8th September 1985)

62

SEPARATED AND REMARRIED COUPLES

God does not stop to love the people who separate themselves in marriage, even the people who live in irregular union. He continues to support these people with the unchanging faithfulness of His love, continually calling attention to the sanctity of the life and, at the same time, urging them not to give up hope. Reflecting, in some way, the love of God, the Church does not exclude from its pastoral concern separated and remarried couples; indeed, the Church provides them with the means of salvation. While maintaining the practice, based on Sacred Scripture, of not admitting the people who are separated and remarried to Eucharistic communion, because their condition of life is objectively opposed to the meaning and ends of the Eucharist, the Church urges them to hear the Word of God, to attend the Sacrifice of the Mass, to persevere in prayer and works of charity, to educate their children in the Christian faith, to cultivate the spirit and practice of penance and thus implore the grace of God and prepare themselves to receive it (*Familiaris Consortio*, No. 84).

The Church is aware of being in the world, with this teaching, "a sign of contradiction".

The prophetic words which Simeon uttered about the Child, Christ, in his life are applied also to the Church in its history. Many times Christ, Gospel and Church become a "sign of contradiction" to the man who is not with "God", but of the world, and even the "prince of darkness". Even calling evil by Its name and absolutely opposed to Him, Christ is always meeting human weakness. He searches the lost sheep. He heals the wounds of the soul. He consoles such people through His cross.

(Pope John Paul II's Homily at Portugal on 15th May 1982)

63

NEW AND YOUNG HOUSES

The pastoral care of the regularly established family signifies, in practice, the commitment of all the members of the local ecclesial community in helping the couple to discover and live their new vocation and mission. In order that the family remains a true community of love, it is necessary that all its members should be helped and trained in their responsibilities as they face the new problems that arise, in mutual service, and in active sharing in family life.

This holds true especially for young families, which, find themselves in context of new values and responsibilities, are more vulnerable, especially in the first years of marriage, to possible difficulties, such as those created by adaptation to life together or by the birth of children. Young married couples should learn to accept willingly, and make good use of, the discreet, tactful and generous help offered by other couples that already have more experience of married and family life. Thus, within the ecclesial community, the great family made up of Christian families, there will take place a mutual exchange of presence and help among all the families, each one putting at the service of others its own experience of life, as well as the gifts of faith and grace. Animated by a true apostolic spirit, this assistance from family to family will constitute one of the simplest, most effective and most accessible means for transmitting from one to another those Christian values which are both the starting point and goal of all pastoral care. Thus, young families will not limit themselves merely to receiving, but in their turn, having been helped in this way, will become a source of enrichment for other longer established families, through their witness of life and practical contribution.

In her pastoral care of young families, the Church must also pay special attention in helping married couple to live responsibly in relationship with its demands of communion and service to life. She must likewise help them to harmonize the intimacy of home life with the generous shared work of building up the Church and Society. When children are born and the married couple becomes a family in the full and specific sense, the Church will still remain close to the parents in order that they may accept their children and love them as a gift received from the Lord of life, and joyfully accept the task of serving them in their human and Christian growth.

(Pope John Paul II, Apostolic Exhortation,
Familiaris Consortio, No. 69)

64

HOUSE MUST BE A PLACE OF EVANGELISATION

Home, Family - Domestic Church - must also be evangelizing. In fact, Christian spouses, through Baptism, confirmation and marriage have to pass on the faith and give the values that transform the society according to the plan of God. They must be convinced that Christ is present in the family, and they must be the most suitable evangelizers of their children. They should transmit their experience of faith with the word, but especially with the daily witness of their newly married life as members of the Church and of Society.

Fathers, you must also be the first catechists and educators of your children in love. If you do not teach to love and pray in the family, then you can hardly fill this void in your family. The life and faith of your children are countless treasures that the Lord has placed in your house. Show to your children the path of good, and accompany them especially in times of difficulty or crisis. Your Christian witness should be the obligatory reference to them to rekindle the flame of their faith and the love you have sown in their hearts. Your evangelization and catechesis in your family must make your family an ecclesial communion. The fathers are expected to be the witnesses in their parishes and families through preaching and genuine Christian catechesis with the right guidance of their pastors.

(Homily of Pope John Paul II at Cali, Colombia on 4th July 1986)

65

FAMILY AND CHURCH

The Christian family is called upon to take part actively and responsibly in the mission of the Church in a way that is original and specific, by placing itself, in what it is and what it does as an "intimate community of life and love," at the service of the Church and of Society.

Since the Christian family is a community in which the relationships are renewed by Christ through faith and the sacraments, the family's sharing in the Church's mission should follow a community pattern: the spouses together as a couple, the parents and children as a family, must live their service to the Church and to the world. They must be "one heart and soul" in faith, through the shared apostolic zeal that animates them, and through their shared commitment to works of service to the ecclesial and civil communities.

The Christian family also builds up the Kingdom of God in history through the everyday realities that concern and distinguish its state of life. It is thus, between husband and wife and between the members of the family-a love lived out in all its extraordinary richness of values and demands: totality, oneness, fidelity and fruitfulness that the Christian family's participation in the prophetic, priestly and kingly mission of Jesus Christ and of His Church finds expression and realization. Therefore, love and life constitute the nucleus of the saving mission of the Christian family in the Church and for the Church.

The Second Vatican Council recalls this fact when it writes: "Families will share their spiritual riches generously with other families too. Thus, the Christian family, which springs from marriage as a reflection of the loving covenant uniting Christ with the Church, and as a participation in that covenant will manifest to all people the saviors, living presence in the world, and the genuine nature of the Church. This the family will do by the mutual love of the spouses, by their generous fruitfulness, their solidarity and faithfulness, and by the loving way in which all the members of the family work together."

Having laid the foundation of the participation of the Christian family in the Church's mission, it is now time to illustrate its substance in reference to Jesus Christ as Prophet, Priest and King - three aspects of a single reality - by presenting the Christian family as 1) a believing and evangelizing community, 2) a community in dialogue with God, and 3) a community at the service of man.

(Pope John Paul II, Apostolic Exhortation,
Familiaris Consortio, No. 50)

66

FAMILY AND SOCIETY

The family is a community of persons and the smallest social unit. As such it is an institution fundamental to the life of every society.

What does the family as an institution expect from society? First of all, it expects recognition of its identity and an acceptance of its status as a subject in society. This social subjectivity is bound up with the proper identity of marriage and the family. Marriage, which makes the institution of the family, is constituted by the covenant whereby a man and a woman establish between themselves a partnership of their whole life, and which of its own very nature is ordered to the well-being of the spouses and to the procreation and upbringing of children. Only such a union can be recognized and ratified as a "marriage" in society. Other interpersonal unions which do not fulfill the above conditions cannot be recognized, despite certain growing trends which represent a serious threat to the future of the family and of society itself.

No human society can run the risk of permissiveness in fundamental issues regarding the nature of marriage and the family. Such moral permissiveness cannot fail to damage the authentic requirements of peace and communion among people. It is thus, quite understandable why the Church vigorously defends the identity of the family and encourages responsible individuals and institutions, especially political leaders and international organizations, not to yield to the temptation of a superficial and false modernity.

As a community of love and life, the family is a firmly grounded social reality. It is also, in a way entirely its own, a sovereign society, although conditioned in certain ways. This affirmation of the family's sovereignty as an institution and the recognition of the various ways in which it is conditioned naturally leads to the subject of family rights. In this regard, the Holy See published in 1983 the Charter of the Rights of the Family; even today this document has lost none of its relevance.

The rights of the family are closely linked to the rights of the person: If in fact the family is a communion of persons, its self-realization will depend in large part on the correct application of the rights of its members. Some of these rights concern the family in an immediate way, such as the right of parents to responsible procreation and the education of children. Other rights, however, touch the family unit only indirectly: Among these, the right to property, especially to what is called family property, and the right to work are of special importance.

But, the rights of the family are not simply the sum total of the rights of the person, since the family is much more than the sum of its individual members. It is a community of parents and children, and at times a community of several generations. For this reason its status as a subject, which is grounded in God's plan, gives rise to and calls for certain proper and specific rights. The Charter of the Rights of the Family, on the basis of the moral principles mentioned above, consolidates the existence of the institution of the family in the social and juridical order of the "greater" society - those of the nation, of the state and of international communities. Each of these greater societies is at least indirectly conditioned by the existence of the family. As a result, the definition of the rights and duties of the greater society with regard to the family is an extremely important and even essential issue.

In the first place, there is the almost organic link existing between the family and the nation. Naturally, we cannot speak in all cases about a nation in the proper sense. Ethnic groups still exist which, without being able to be considered true nations, do fulfill to some extent the function of a greater society. In both cases, the link of the family with the ethnic group or the nation is founded above all on a participation in its culture. In one sense, parents also give birth to children for the nation so that they can be members of it and can share in its historic and cultural heritage. From the very outset the identity of the family is to some extent shaped by the identity of the nation to which it belongs.

By sharing in the nation's cultural heritage, the family contributes to that specific sovereignty which has its origin in a distinct culture and language. I addressed this subject at the UNESCO conference meeting in Paris in 1980, and, given its unquestionable importance, I have often returned to it. Not only the nations, but every family realizes its spiritual sovereignty through culture and language. Were this not true, it would be very difficult to explain many events in the history of peoples, especially in Europe. From these events, ancient and modern, inspiring and painful, glorious and humiliating, it becomes clear how much the family is an organic part of the nation and the nation of the family.

With regard to the State the link with the family is somewhat similar and at the same time somewhat dissimilar. The State, in fact, is distinct from the nation; it has a less family like structure, since it is organized in accordance with a political system and in a more bureaucratic fashion. None the less, the apparatus of the State also has, in some sense, a soul of its own, to the extent that it lives up to its nature as a political community juridically ordered toward the common good. Closely linked to this soul is the family, which is connected with the State precisely by reason of the Principle of Subsidiarity. Indeed, the family is a social reality which does not have readily available all the means necessary to carry out its proper ends, also in matters regarding schooling and the rearing of children. The State is thus, called upon to play a role in accordance with the principle mentioned above. Whenever the family is self-sufficient, it should be left to act on its own; an excessive intrusiveness on the part of the State would prove detrimental, lacking due respect, and would constitute an open violation of the rights of the family. Only in those situations where the family is not really self-sufficient does the State have the authority and duty to intervene.

Beyond child rearing and schooling at all levels, State assistance, while not excluding private initiatives, can find expression in institutions such as those founded to safeguard the life and health of citizens, and in particular to provide social benefits for workers. Unemployment is today one of the most serious threats to family life and a rightful cause of concern to every society. It represents a challenge for the political life of individual States and an area for careful study in the Church's social doctrine. It is urgently necessary, therefore, to come up with courageous solutions capable of looking beyond the confines of one's own nation and taking into consideration the many families for whom lack of employment means living in situations of tragic poverty.

While speaking about employment in reference to the family, it is appropriate to emphasize how important and burdensome is the work women do within the family unit: that work should be acknowledged and deeply appreciated. The toil of a woman who, having given birth to a child, nourishes and cares for that child and devotes herself to its upbringing, particularly in the early years, is so great as to be comparable to any professional work. This ought to be clearly stated and upheld, no less than any other labor right. Motherhood, because of all the hard work it entails, should be recognized as giving the right to financial benefits at least equal to those of other kinds of work undertaken in order to support the family during such a delicate phase of its life.

Every effort should be made so that the family will be recognized as the primordial and, in a certain sense sovereign society. The sovereignty of the family is essential for the good of society. A truly sovereign and spiritually vigorous nation is always made up of strong families who are aware of their vocation and mission in history. The family is at the heart of all these problems and tasks. To relegate it to a subordinate or secondary role, excluding it from its rightful position in society would be to inflict grave harm on the authentic growth of society as a whole.

(Pope John Paul II's Letter to Families on 2nd February 1994)

67

CHARTER OF THE RIGHTS OF THE FAMILY

Realizing the essential importance of family life for a just and healthy society, the Holy See has presented a Charter of the Rights of the Family based on the natural rights and values common to all humanity. It is addressed principally to Governments and International Organizations, as a "model and point of reference for the drawing up of legislation and family policy, and guidance for action programmes".

Among the principles which the Church vigorously upholds in every circumstance there are the following, which I call to your attention:

- the inalienable right of spouses to found a family and to decide on the spacing of births and the number of children to be born, taking into full consideration their duties towards themselves, their children already born, the family and society, in a just hierarchy of values and in accordance with the objective moral order . . .;
- all pressures brought to bear in limiting "the freedom of couples in deciding about children constitute a grave offence against human dignity and justice";

- "families have the right to be able to rely on an adequate family policy on the part of public authorities in the juridical, economic, social and fiscal domains, without any discrimination whatsoever".

(Homily of Pope John Paul II at Perth, Australia on 30th November 1987)

68

SPIRITUAL DISORIENTATION THREATENS FAMILIES

Mary's cooperation in the mystery of God's plan as it is unfolded in the Incarnation of her Son invites all Christian parents and children to think about their own vocation to be *cooperators in the mystery of God's grace at work within their families.* Our faith teaches us that each *human life,* beginning at the moment of conception, is a *gift from the Creator* and endowed with an infinite value in his eyes. Our faith reminds us that all human beings have been created in God's own image and likeness and given a vocation and destiny that will find their ultimate fulfillment beyond this earthly existence, in a communion of life and love with the Blessed Trinity. Faith also teaches us that we are united with all other members of the human race in a *deep moral solidarity,* that our actions and choices have consequences not only for ourselves but for others, and that we shall be judged by the measure of our love and concern atleast for our brothers and sisters.

Is it not in the life of their families that most people come to learn the magnificent truth which lies behind these profound affirmations of Christian faith? Unfortunately, it is easy for individuals and families to be so caught up in the many anxieties of daily life that they fail to stand back, put their lives in spiritual perspective, and rediscover the truth of their own vocation. How tragic this is, for without a spirit of prayer and meditation how can we discern God's will for us, turn to him in obedience and love, and thus experience the happiness and peace for which he created us?

For this reason, I encourage all of you to *pray constantly* (I Thes 5:17), especially within your families, in humble thanksgiving for everything that God in his goodness has done for you. Ask him every day to help you *to remain faithful to the vocation which he has given you in Christ*. Do not be afraid to bring before Him all your hopes, your needs and concerns. Parents, pray for your children, that they may grow in the new life which they received in Baptism. Children, pray for your parents, for you too have a part to play in making them Holy (*Gaudium et Spes*, No. 48). Moreover, as members of a greater family, pray in union with Christ's Body throughout the world *for the needs of all humanity*: for the sick and the oppressed, for the leaders of nations, for those who labor for justice and peace among people, and for those who promote responsible stewardship of the natural environment. Pray for all those who in any way give glory to God by humbly serving the needs of their brothers and sisters. And whether your work is at home, in the fields or at sea, in the factories or in Malta's growing tourist industry, offer it to the Lord as a pleasing sacrifice in preparation for the coming of His kingdom.

(Pope John Paul II's Homily at Malta on 26th May 1990)

69

MEDIA AND FAMILY

RISK AND RICHNESS

Thanks to the unprecedented expansion of the communications market in recent decades, many families throughout the world, even those of quite modest means, now have access in their own homes to immense and varied media resources. As a result, they enjoy virtually unlimited opportunities for information, education, cultural expansion, and even spiritual growth - opportunities that far exceed those available to most families in earlier times.

Yet these same media also have the capacity to do grave harm to families by presenting an inadequate or even deformed outlook on life, on the family, on religion, and on morality. This power either to reinforce or override traditional values like religion, culture, and family was clearly seen by the Second Vatican Council, which taught that "if the media are to be correctly employed, it is essential that all who use them know the principles of the moral order, and apply them faithfully" (*Inter Mirifica*, No. 4). Communication in any form must always be inspired by the ethical criterion of respect for the truth and for the dignity of the human person.

The family and the family life are all too often inadequately portrayed in the media. Infidelity, sexual activity outside the marriage, and the absence of a moral and spiritual vision of the marriage covenant are depicted uncritically, while positive support is at times given to divorce, contraception, abortion, and homosexuality. Such portrayals, by promoting causes inimical to marriage and the family, are detrimental to the common good of society.

Conscientious reflection on the ethical dimension of communications should issue in practical initiatives aimed at eliminating the risks to the well-being of the family posed by the media, and that these powerful instruments of communication will remain genuine sources of enrichment. A special responsibility in this regard lies with communicators themselves, with public authorities, and with parents.

It is not so easy to resist commercial pressures or the demands of conformity to secular ideologies, but that is what responsible communicators must do. The stakes are high, since every attack on the fundamental value of the family is an attack on the true good of humanity.

Public authorities themselves have a serious duty to uphold marriage and the family for the sake of society itself. Instead, many now accept and act upon the unsound libertarian arguments of groups which advocate practices which contribute to the grave phenomenon of family crisis and the weakening of the very concept of the family. Without resorting to censorship, it is imperative that public authorities set in place regulatory policies and procedures to ensure that the media do not act against the good of the family. Family representatives should be part of this policy-making.

Parents also need to regulate the use of media in the home. This would include planning and scheduling media use, strictly limiting the time children devote to media, making entertainment a family experience, putting some media entirely off limits, and periodically excluding all of them for the sake of other family activities. Above all, parents should give good example to children by their own thoughtful and selective use of media.

The media of social communications have an enormous positive potential for promoting sound human and family values, and thus contributing to the renewal of society. In view of their great power to shape ideas and influence behavior, professional communicators should recognize that they have a moral responsibility not only to give families all possible encouragement, assistance, and support to that end, but also to exercise wisdom, good judgment, and fairness in their presentation of issues involving sexuality, marriage, and family life.

(Message of Pope John Paul II on the World Communications Day on 24th January 2004)

CONCLUSION

Finally, you are worried to see many young people, brides and bridegrooms who keep distance themselves from the Church for reasons of sexual ethics.

The moral requirements are clearly part of the sexuality and these are the consequences of the faith in the Gospel. It is also true in terms of charity, social justice. The ethics of family life is important, although some people try to relegate it. We must not be afraid of recalling these moral requirements, of underlining the abnormal situations of sin. All the Christians should be able to understand these requirements. However, we must expose to them more than as mere rules and regulations; the beauty and the richness of the Christian values are to be made known to them. Is not the teaching of the Church on marriage and sexuality capable of leading the newlyweds to form a good family and society?

But today, the Christian faith is in question, the sense of sin has diminished and the authority of the Church is not accepted with confidence. More generally when you want to speak to a large audience, consisting of Christians and Non-Christians, especially through the media, it is true that we cannot remember only the injunctions of morality. We will be rejected in the name of certain liberalism. We must, with clear language, explain a healthy theology of the body without giving up the ethics; we need to promote the values of true human love and respect for life. Genuine love emerges from the moral requirements. It is important that this love finds its place in families and in society. The family must maintain, reveal and communicate the true love. A society cannot be built without these values and it will decay if it abandons these values.

So, we should not give up our teaching in the context in which family morality is denied and absolute freedom without the responsibility of love and of human life is promoted. We must always involve in the debate, with the help of many men and women of good will, at least for the good of society, for the dignity and the eternal happiness of people. We hope that the pastors, lay Christians and the associations do their best to educate people and accompany, with all appropriate initiatives, those who are trying to learn, to progress. It is a journey of hope.

(Address of Pope John Paul II to the
Bishops of France on 9th October 1982)

PRAYER OF JOHN PAUL II FOR FAMILIES

Lord God, from You every family in Heaven and on earth takes its name. Father, You are love and life.

Through Your Son, Jesus Christ, born of woman, and through the Holy Spirit, the fountain of divine charity, grant that every family on earth may become for each successive generation a true shrine of life and love.

Grant that Your grace may guide the thoughts and actions of husbands and wives for the good of their families and of all the families in the world.

Grant that the young may find in the family solid support for their human dignity and for their growth in truth and love.

Grant that love, strengthened by the grace of the sacrament of marriage, may prove mightier than all the weaknesses and trials through which our families sometimes pass.

Through the intercession of the Holy Family of Nazareth, grant that the Church may fruitfully carry out her worldwide mission in the family and through the family.

We ask this of You, Who is life, truth and love with the Son and the Holy Spirit. Amen.

INDEX

THE BOOK

Marriage is one of the oldest human traditions. The union of man and woman creates a new cell and both unite in a lawful and social relation to set up a family. Family is the nucleus of the society and its happiness depends on the well preparation for marriage. The marriage is not a simple ceremony or it is not for satisfaction of sexual urge. Unity and indissolubility are the essential properties of marriage. With children born of marital union, the couple finds a paradise in the house. The children bring to the family joy, prosperity and unity. Unfortunately the value of marriage and family is underestimated in many societies, especially in the Western societies. Saint John Paul II who is also called as the Father of the Families had unceasingly fought for the protection of value of marriage and family through his conferences, homilies and talks. He visited all parts of the world, encountered different groups of people and insisted on the responsibility of each and every one to protect the institution of marriage and family. This book is a collection of his thoughts delivered on various occasions.

THE AUTHOR

Dr. Sahayaraj Lourdusamy, Priest of the Diocese of Thanjavur, Tamil Nadu, is the member of the High Council of AIDOP Commission of Paris (*Agence international diplomatie et opinion publique*) and is the Research Scholar of the Asian Department of Canon Law and Culture of the Faculty of Canon Law, Catholic Institute of Paris. Besides his Master's degree in Sociology, Computer Science and Journalism and Bachelor's Degree in Mathematics, Education and Indian Civil Law, he holds a doctorate in Canon Law from the Catholic Institute of Paris and also a doctorate in Civil Law from the University of Paris XI, France. He has authored 7 books in Tamil, 2 books in French and 1 book in English. At present he is the Chancellor of the Diocese of Thanjavur and one of the Judges in the Diocesan Tribunal.